12.74

D0201185

The Land and People of
HUNGARY

The people of Hungary, a remarkably resilient nation, have managed to hold onto their heritage for over a thousand years, despite long periods of domination by many different powers. Settled around 900 by the Magyars, the land was invaded by Mongols, ruled by Turks, and subsequently joined to Austria. Hungary fought on the losing side in both world wars and was then drawn into the Soviet orbit by the victorious sweep of the Russian armies across Eastern Europe in 1945. The political and economic life of today's Hungary is still shaped by this connection. Emil Lengyel has brought his study of Hungary and its people up to date with an account of recent developments in Hungary under the present regime.

PORTRAITS OF THE NATIONS SERIES

THE LAND AND PEOPLE OF AFGHANISTAN

THE LAND AND PEOPLE OF ALGERIA

THE LAND AND PEOPLE OF ARGENTINA

THE LAND AND PEOPLE OF AUSTRALIA

THE LAND AND PEOPLE OF AUSTRIA

THE LAND AND PEOPLE OF THE BALKANS

THE LAND AND PEOPLE OF BELGIUM

THE LAND AND PEOPLE OF BOLIVIA

THE LAND AND PEOPLE OF BRAZIL

THE LAND AND PEOPLE OF BURMA

THE LAND AND PEOPLE OF CAMBODIA

THE LAND AND PEOPLE OF CANADA

THE LAND AND PEOPLE OF CENTRAL AMERICA

THE LAND AND PEOPLE OF CEYLON

THE LAND AND PEOPLE OF CHILE

THE LAND AND PEOPLE OF CHINA

THE LAND AND PEOPLE OF COLOMBIA

THE LAND AND PEOPLE OF THE CONGO

THE LAND AND PEOPLE OF CUBA

THE LAND AND PEOPLE OF CZECHOSLOVAKIA

THE LAND AND PEOPLE OF DENMARK

THE LAND AND PEOPLE OF EGYPT

THE LAND AND PEOPLE OF ENGLAND

THE LAND AND PEOPLE OF ETHIOPIA

THE LAND AND PEOPLE OF FINLAND

THE LAND AND PEOPLE OF FRANCE

THE LAND AND PEOPLE OF GERMANY

THE LAND AND PEOPLE OF GHANA

THE LAND AND PEOPLE OF GREECE

THE LAND AND PEOPLE OF THE GUIANAS

THE LAND AND PEOPLE OF HOLLAND

THE LAND AND PEOPLE OF HUNGARY

THE LAND AND PEOPLE OF ICELAND

THE LAND AND PEOPLE OF INDIA

THE LAND AND PEOPLE OF INDONESIA

THE LAND AND PEOPLE OF IRAN

THE LAND AND PEOPLE OF IRAQ

THE LAND AND PEOPLE OF IRELAND

THE LAND AND PEOPLE OF ISRAEL

THE LAND AND PEOPLE OF ITALY

THE LAND AND PEOPLE OF JAPAN

THE LAND AND PEOPLE OF JORDAN

THE LAND AND PEOPLE OF KENYA

THE LAND AND PEOPLE OF KOREA

THE LAND AND PEOPLE OF LEBANON

THE LAND AND PEOPLE OF LIBERIA

THE LAND AND PEOPLE OF LIBYA

THE LAND AND PEOPLE OF MALAYSIA

THE LAND AND PEOPLE OF MEXICO

THE LAND AND PEOPLE OF MOROCCO

THE LAND AND PEOPLE OF NEW ZEALAND

THE LAND AND PEOPLE OF NIGERIA

THE LAND AND PEOPLE OF NORWAY

THE LAND AND PEOPLE OF PAKISTAN

THE LAND AND PEOPLE OF PERU

THE LAND AND PEOPLE OF THE PHILIPPINES

THE LAND AND PEOPLE OF POLAND

THE LAND AND PEOPLE OF PORTUGAL

THE LAND AND PEOPLE OF RHODESIA

THE LAND AND PEOPLE OF ROMANIA

THE LAND AND PEOPLE OF RUSSIA

THE LAND AND PEOPLE OF SCOTLAND

THE LAND AND PEOPLE OF SIERRA LEONE

THE LAND AND PEOPLE OF SOUTH AFRICA

THE LAND AND PEOPLE OF SPAIN

THE LAND AND PEOPLE OF SWEDEN

THE LAND AND PEOPLE OF SYRIA

THE LAND AND PEOPLE OF TANZANIA

THE LAND AND PEOPLE OF THAILAND

THE LAND AND PEOPLE OF TUNISIA

THE LAND AND PEOPLE OF TURKEY

THE LAND AND PEOPLE OF URUGUAY

THE LAND AND PEOPLE OF VENEZUELA

THE LAND AND PEOPLE OF THE WEST INDIES

THE LAND AND PEOPLE OF ZAMBIA

Also in the same format

THE ISLAND OF PUERTO RICO

The Land and People of
HUNGARY

by Emil Lengyel

PORTRAITS OF THE NATIONS SERIES

J. B. LIPPINCOTT COMPANY
Philadelphia   New York

To
Gretchen and Peter
for a lifetime of happiness

U. S. Library of Congress Cataloging in Publication Data

Lengyel, Emil, birth date
  The land and people of Hungary.

  (Portraits of the nations series)
  SUMMARY: Surveys briefly the urban and rural life, history, and
folk customs of the country whose people say it is the flower on the
hat of God.

  1. Hungary—Juvenile literature. [1. Hungary] I. Title.
DB925.3.L45   1972   914.39   72-37763
ISBN-0-397-31545-7 TSE Ed.

MAP BY DONALD T. PITCHER

The author wishes to thank the following for their kind permission
to use the photographs on the following pages:

Eastfoto: 31, 90, 98, 102, 112, 117, 119, 126, 135, 146, 147.
Hungarian Telegraphic Agency: 136, 137. Hungarian Telegraphic
Agency and Legation of the Hungarian People's Republic: 10, 109.
Legation of the Hungarian People's Republic: 123, 152.

ACKNOWLEDGMENTS

MY THANKS to Helen Wallace whose editorial perspicacity suggested welcome improvements; and to Sonya Polonsky for the zeal she displayed in selecting illustrative material.

My gratitude to Marie Kirkpatrick, whose devotion to work in the social science department of Fairleigh Dickinson University, Rutherford, N.J. enabled me to have the time for writing.

Many thanks, also, to a dear friend of my youth, Erno Sebestyen, in speeding illustrative material to me across the seas, and to Bela Szathmary, for the insights into the operation of a bewildering system. I am also thankful to Jozsef Kelemen, farm manager in the village of Tura on the Galga River, who helped me gain a better understanding of complex farm problems.

CONTENTS

The Danube, near Visegrad.

1

This Is the Land

"IF THE earth is the hat of God, Hungary is the flower on it," Hungarian children used to sing. Hungarian adults had the habit of saying, only half in fun: "Whenever God talks, He speaks Hungarian."

The Hungarian's great pride in his country helps to compensate for the countless humiliations he has endured. Powerful neighbors surround him; Hungary has been invaded and occupied by Russians, Germans, and Tartars, by Austrians and Turks. Intruders from near and far have tried to pluck "the flower on God's hat," but the Hungarian has held his own, and so he likes to boast.

Hungary is a small country now; it would take a hundred Hungaries to fill the space occupied by the United

States. It has thirty-five thousand square miles of land, inhabited by more than ten million people. Although small, Hungary has filled more chapters of history texts and more newspaper headlines than countries many times its size, and for excellent reasons.

A notable reason for the importance of Hungary is its location in the lush mid-Danubian region of Europe, one of the most desirable farmlands on earth. Much of its soil is black earth, "humus," which compares favorably with the choicest farmland in the American Middle West.

Also, Hungary occupies a region of great strategic importance. The Danube, nature's great gift to Hungary, provides a natural highway for would-be conquerors as well as a natural boundary.

The Danube was the easternmost frontier of ancient Rome against the barbarians. When Rome's power declined, looting Eastern hordes tried to establish themselves in this rich land. The Tartars of the thirteenth century fought for the Middle Danube; they were followed by Turks in the sixteenth century; when the Turkish Empire collapsed, Hapsburg power penetrated into Hungary. In the two World Wars of this century, Germany had to secure the Hungarian pivot before she could strike out against the Russians. In turn, Russia knew that she could control Eastern Europe only if she could hold on to Hungary.

The frontiers of modern Hungary were drawn after the First World War. For over a thousand years before that catastrophe, it was a much larger country. Today its boundaries are close to its capital. Budapest is only an hour's drive from Czechoslovakia in the north, three hours' drive from Yugoslavia in the south, another three hours' drive west from Austria. In the east the distance is longer; it is five hours' drive from Budapest to the Rumanian border.

The Danube (called *Duna* by the Hungarians) originates in Germany's Black Forest and flows for 1,750 miles through Austria, Hungary, Yugoslavia, and Rumania before it reaches the Black Sea. The Danube is a "horizontal" stream during most of its course, flowing from West to East; only in Hungary does it become "vertical," flowing from North to South. Hence, the various parts of the country are oriented toward the river. The rolling land to the west, reaching out toward Austria, is known as Trans-Danube. The country to the east is called Cis-Danube. The capital of the country, Budapest, is divided by the Danube

The Danube, as it divides Budapest.

into two cities; Buda on the right bank, Pest on the left.

The Danube sustains many of the nation's most important industries, and provides cheap transportation and waterpower. It forms part of the frontier between Hungary and Czechoslovakia. It is a great transcontinental highway, Hungary's strongest link with the West.

The world has come to know the stream as "the beautiful blue Danube," the title of the best-known waltz of Johann Strauss. It is beautiful, indeed, but it is not blue. It has become brown, as its waves keep lapping at the fertile soil of the banks. Some of its tributaries have a milky sheen, which gets lost in the ochre color of the main stream.

Along many miles of its course, the Danube is flanked by reeds and flowers. The scent of the flowers, of the trees on the banks, and of the river itself produces an air which sweetens the countryside. The small streams which join the Danube in Hungary are bordered with weeping willows and inhabited by herons. The bullfrogs and the little river steamers lend their characteristic tones to the concert of the Danube.

The stretch of the Danube which divides Hungary and Czechoslovakia does not separate two different worlds, and the landscapes are similar on both banks. There are villages, farmhouses, and pleasant agricultural land, its fresh green fading into the pastel-colored sky. In this rural setting it is easy to forget that factory districts are not far from either bank.

Passengers on the Vienna-to-Budapest steamer have an opportunity to see a great deal of the countryside of the river. First, the slim spire of a village church floats into view, creating the illusion that it is floating on a wave of tall corn. Then the village itself passes in review. The red tiles of the roofs of the squat houses contrast pleasantly with the blue sky and the dun-colored grain. The church occupies the center of town, and houses cluster around it as if for protection.

As the steamer moves along into mid-Danubia, one of the problems of the region is made plain. There is a city here, a Danubian city—one part of it on the left bank, in Czechoslovakia; one part on the right bank, in Hungary. The city has two names; Komarno in Czechoslovakia, Komarom in Hungary. Until the end of the first World War, it was one (Hungarian) city; after the war, it was just one casualty in the reduction of Hungary, which once reached hundreds of miles north to the Carpathians.

History casts a long shadow over this part of the Danube. Centuries ago, old Komarom was reputed to be the strongest fortress in Europe. The Turks besieged the city four times in a single century; and when they were gone, the Hapsburg armies came. The city was considered so impregnable that the treasures of the Hapsburg dynasty were hidden there during the Napoleonic Wars. Half a century later, during the Austro-Prussian War of 1866, the gold holdings of the Vienna National Bank were sent there for safekeeping. Komarom made history again during the uprising against the Communists in 1956. Many of the industrial workers of the city made a determined attempt to overturn their despotic government.

As the steamer passenger continues his journey along the Danube, he may remember and wonder about sights

A reconstructed castle in Budapest.

seen on other river journeys. Where are the castles along the Hungarian Danube? On the Austrian Danube, there are many—a procession of ruined castles passes in review under the eyes of the traveler. On the Rhine, every twist of the stream reveals a new fort or castle, all of them picturesque. But here the river is short of castles.

The Danube does not lack for castles because it lacked for armies. On the contrary, it was the very highway of the invaders. There were forts on the Hungarian mid-Danube, too, but they were swept away by centuries of invasion and war.

The great river is wrapped in silence for much of its length. Occasionally one hears the panting of the upstream ships, pulled by a string of tugs, but for long stretches, there is quiet. The Danube is a much larger river than the Rhine, but the Rhine has long carried much heavier traffic. In the "normal" years before World War II, the Rhine carried eighty-five million tons annually, in contrast to the seven million tons on the Danube.

There is heavy traffic on the Rhine because it carries the products of much larger industries than are found in Hungary, and it takes these products to eager consumers. Danubian traffic has to cross the Iron Curtain separating the West from the Communist countries. It has to cross, too, the "Iron Gate" in Rumania, where the smooth course of the river is interrupted by the Transylvanian Alps.

Then, too, the Danube flows from West to East, against the flow of normal European traffic. The affluent Western nations, with their large purchasing power, are at the "wrong" end of the river. The East was for many years a raw-material producing region, with only limited ability to use or pay for the high-priced industrial products of the West.

Finally, the Rhine flows into the North Sea, which hums with the trade not only of Europe, but of North America. The Black Sea, destination of the Danube, is not nearly as busy. Goods carried into that sea must pass through the Turkish Straits to find richer markets, and even then, in most cases, the cargo has not reached its ultimate destination.

The passenger on the Danube steamer, reflecting on the peaceful course of the river after Komarom-Komarno, is startled by an apparition. He sees a huge church which seems to float on air, and it is not a mirage. It is St. Peter's on the Danube, a replica of the Roman basilica, the most majestic cathedral in the world. The Hungarian St. Peter's is the seat of the Primate Cardinal Archbishop of Hungary in the city of Esztergom, the "Vatican" of Hungary.

St. Peter's is a massive and magnificent cathedral. Its six-foot-thick walls remind us that it served as a fortress at one time. Esztergom was the capital of the country during the reign of the Arpad dynasty, the first ruling house of Hungary.

At Esztergom, hills interrupt the flat scenery of the mid-Danube. They form a narrow loop and serve as a bridge between the Carpathian Mountains far to the North and the outlying foothills of the Alps in the West. Some of these hills shelter world-famous vineyards.

A few miles east of Esztergom the hills force the river to change course, and the Danube executes a bold right turn. The "horizontal" becomes "vertical" for about 230 miles, entirely within Hungary. This vertical stretch of river boasts a cluster of historic spots, royal castles, dungeons, and strong points.

These include the ruins of the royal palace of Visegrad. For a brief period Visegrad was the royal seat during the Middle Ages. The ruins are on promontories on the right bank, underneath tree-covered hills. The citadel of the palace had the picturesque name of "Fellegvar"— Cloud Castle. There was kept Hungary's greatest treasure, the "Holy Crown" which conferred supreme authority on the anointed king. Among the ruins is a dungeon whose inmates must have trembled before the king's near-divine power.

The ruins of the Cloud Castle at Visegrad.

Budapest is not very far from Visegrad. To the north of the capital, on the right bank, are the remains of a military camp of the ancient Romans. Scholars say that the name of the camp, Aquincum, indicates that the camp may even pre-date the Romans. "Aquincum" is derived from the Celtic phrase *Ak-Ink,* meaning "abundant waters."

The Roman camp on the Danube was just one of that great empire's outposts on the rivers of Europe. Roman legions on the Rhine and on the Danube stood at the boundaries of civilization as they knew it; their soldiers faced the barbarians of West and East from the great rivers which defined the empire. A Roman legionary must have faced a tour of duty in Budapest with very much the emotions of a modern American soldier stationed in northern-most Alaska.

Excavations in Aquincum revealed a high degree of civilization in the camp. There were public baths, a sewer, theaters for games and plays, a forum for law courts and for public discussion, and sanctuaries for the many gods of Rome.

Local tradition has named numerous mounds all over the country "Roman palisades." They may be, or they could be vestiges of some barbarian occupation. Along the river, at strategic points, the Roman legions maintained outposts. They had a fort at Arrabona, which is the city of Gyor today, and at Sopianae, near Pecs, lower down the stream. On the whole, few traces of the Roman outposts have been dug out in Hungary. The countless wars throughout the centuries wiped out even the memory of them.

"The Scourge of God," the formidable leader of the Huns, Attila, is believed to have maintained one of his headquarters near Budapest. Indeed, Buda is said to have been his brother's name.

Civilization, and the lack of it, has had a long history along the majestic stream.

2

On the Plains and in the Hills

Is THERE a typical Hungarian countryside? Of course not, because nothing in nature is typical, but certain regions do have specific characteristics. The two banks of the Danube have separate qualities which can be observed quite distinctly by a traveler making his way along the great river. To the west is Transdanubia and its rolling hills, the hills which roll all the way to the Alps and the West. To the east are plains which extend all the way to the Transylvanian hills of Rumania.

All along the river are farmlands, wheat and corn, truck gardens. Certainly this land is not poor in natural resources, nor in the problems these resources imply. All through Hungary's history the countryside was too rich to

21

be left in peace. Therefore it has been subjected to repeated invasions and migrations from east and west. Again and again, Hungary has been depopulated by war, its people replaced by victorious invaders or new groups of farmers.

Kiskunsag is the name of the eastern region—Little Cumania, bearing the name of the nomadic tribe of the *Kun,* known also as *Polovtsi* or *Kipchaks.* Centuries ago, the Kun settled on this rich land, already depopulated by many wars. The Asian Cuman heritage may account for the dark eyes seen in this area. The descendants of the Kun are now old Hungarians; they have inhabited this soil for centuries.

A row of towns follow the river south of Budapest— Paks, Szekszard, Baja, and others, flanked by factory chimneys and blocks of new residential buildings. Industries attract country people and the new city dwellers have to be lodged in apartments. Each of these towns has its history, often a cycle of invasion, destruction, and reconstruction.

Passing the little town of Mohacs, scene of the defeat of the Hungarians by the Turks in the Mohacs Disaster of 1526, the traveler faces the Yugoslavian frontier. At this point he leaves the Danube and enters Transdanubia, a region of great natural variety. Many parts of Transdanubia are hilly, and the hills roll all the way to the foothills of the Austrian Alps. The Bakony Hills, in the center of the Transdanubian range, have an especially romantic history. These heavily wooded hills were the headquarters of Sandor Rozsa, the Hungarian Robin Hood of the nineteenth century, a "kind-hearted robber" who stole from the

Lake Balaton, with the Abbey of Tihany in the background.

rich to help the poor. In the process, he became rich himself.

The hills surround the largest lake in Hungary, one of the largest in Europe—Lake Balaton. Fifty miles long, it is the vacation center of the country. Its southern shore holds Hungary's most popular resort, Siofok; its northern shore presents a dramatic spectacle, ornamented by the old monastery at Tihany. At the end of the lake is Keszthely, a cultural center which attracts gifted musicians.

Lake Balaton is famous for its storms and its uncertain temper. At one moment the water can be as smooth as a mirror; at the next, it is frothing and churning in wild waves, sending the vacationers scuttling back to shore. The lake is known for its wealth of unusual fish, including the perch-pike which makes *halaszle,* the fishermen's broth, a popular dish.

Continuous hills, often segments of the same range, accompany the traveler in many parts of Hungary. They are broken into groups, interspersed with narrow plains, so the various sections have their own intriguing names such as Vertes (Iron-Clad), Dunazug (Danubian Rock), and Pilis. The Pilis Hills force the river to change the direction of its flow from west to south.

Crossing the Danube to the east brings us to Cis-Danubia, which includes most of the country and extends to Transylvania. Here the range of mountains continues in a northeasterly direction, linking the Alpine system of the west with the Carpathians of the north and east. From their peaks, one can look into Czechoslovakia. Part of this region is rich in coal, and the town of Salgotarjan is the center of an important mining area. Miskolc, the second largest city of Hungary, is here. Situated as it is along the main railway line to the Soviet Union, it has become an important industrial and transportation center.

One of the specialties of Hungary is the famous Tokaj wine, named for a small town in this area. Tokaj has a population of not much more than five thousand, but its name is known to the world for its "nectar of the kings." Not far away is another famous wine-growing region, Eger, which produces "bikaver." This is a curious name for a wine; it means "bull's blood," for its purplish-red color. Eger is visited, too, for its ruins of an old fortification which held out against the Turks long after most of Hungary had succumbed.

As the traveler proceeds into the *Nagyalfold,* the Great Plains, he might well believe himself in the American West. It is a flat region of some of the best agricultural land in the country, producing a large variety of farm products and known as an important part of the "breadbasket" of the Danube.

Not all of the land has always been productive. There are areas of poor soil, and there have been dust bowls. The names of some of the towns reveal problems: for instance, "Sar Ret," or "muddy meadow." One of the rivers is named Sebeskoros from the word "sebes," or "rapid." This river and others are tributaries of the largest stream of

The village of Tokaj, famous for its wine.

the Great Plains, the Tisza, which is itself a tributary of the Danube. These rapid streams brought devastation to the area many times as spring thaws released the tremendous force of untamed waters. Now, however, the rivers are being restrained by man.

Large plains exposed to long spells of summer sunshine frequently permit the optical illusion known as a mirage. As the soil is overheated, the lower layers of the air serve as refractors, magnifying objects far beyond their normal size. In the Nagyalfold, a peasant near the edge of the horizon becomes a giant bestriding the world, and a placid cow looks like a prehistoric monster. The smooth asphalt road seems to be flooded with water.

The great city of Debrecen is situated right in the heart of this farm country. Debrecen grew as its inhabitants built sturdy walls to keep out hungry invaders, and its people grew stiff-necked, with a strong feeling of independence. When the Reformation came to Hungary, Debrecen went Calvinist. The Counter-Reformation reconverted most of the country, but not Debrecen. In the midst of Catholic Hungary it has remained a Protestant city, known as the "Calvinist Rome." In the great Calvinist church at Debrecen in 1849 the assembled representatives of Hungary declared the Hapsburg emperor deposed. The deposition did not last long, but it was a bold deed, well in keeping with the rebellious spirit of the city.

Szeged, which was the second largest city in Hungary before the First World War, is on the banks of the river Tisza, in the midst of a particularly fertile section. After World War I, Szeged lost its hinterland to both Yugoslavia and Rumania. It is a pleasant city, with theaters, concerts, museums, and libraries. Its open-air summer theater is known throughout the land.

One of the largest towns in the farm belt has played a roundabout role in the cultural history of America. The name of the town is Mako, and its specialty is onions! Mako was the birthplace of Joseph Pulitzer, one of the Hungarians who migrated from the Hungarian Great Plains to the American Great Plains, and thence to New York. He was a father of modern popular journalism and he established the most coveted literary prize in the United States. The newspaper he operated was the *New York World*, and the prize is the Pulitzer Prize.

Mako is one of the "peasant towns" of the Hungarian plains, one of many which have long served as marketing centers for the farms. Today they are changing and acquiring new industries, but the changes have not affected their serene, staid air. Life in the Hungarian countryside cannot be hurried; people still like to sip wine and listen to music.

The traveler through the main regions of Hungary has observed, above all else, the country's wealth of agricultural resources. The following geographical factors are responsible for this fertility.

Hungary is more than a thousand miles from the Atlantic Ocean; Budapest is about as far from that ocean as St. Louis, Missouri is. The Adriatic, to the south, is the nearest sea, and it is several hundred miles away. Hungary is a landlocked country.

Continental climates run to great extremes of temperature, to intense heat and intense cold. Large land surfaces react quickly to the influence of the sun. Large bodies of water temper these extremes, they retain the heat of the sun for long periods and release its warmth gradually.

Hungary is much farther north than St. Louis; it is between the latitudes of North Dakota and Canada. In northern North Dakota, the winter temperature may drop to −30° F.; in the summer it may shoot up beyond 100° F. This is a typical continental climate.

In spite of Hungary's mid-continental position, her climate is not at all like that of North Dakota, where the prevailing winds blow from west to east. North Dakota gets its frigid air from northern Canada, Alaska, and Siberia. Hungary's prevailing winds originate in the Gulf Stream, which is warm, and the western part of the country, in particular, benefits from them. For that reason, eastern Hungary is colder in winter, warmer in summer than the west, more like typical continental weather.

Hungary also gets some of its weather from the south, and the southern air has a warming influence even though it has to cross many mountain ranges before it reaches the middle Danube. Occasionally the wind turns, and then Hungarians have a taste of a Siberian winter. But this does not happen often, and the Danube at Budapest is frozen over very seldom. The winter begins early, but it is over by mid-March and is followed by the best part of the year— the flower-scented Hungarian spring.

Hungary is near the borderline of the maritime and continental climates. The weather of western Hungary, more like a maritime climate, is moderate; while eastern Hungary is closer to the extremes of temperature characteristic of a continental climate.

The Gulf clouds of the Atlantic are filled with the rain which has made Ireland the Emerald Isle, but not much of the Gulf rain can reach Hungary. Budapest is known to the tourists for its beautiful blue sky. The blue sky means danger for the farmer, though, and great disaster used to follow dry summers. Nowadays, irrigation helps to prevent the calamity of drought, and Hungary's rivers have salvaged many parts of the country which were once too dry to farm.

Occasionally one of the rivers of the country goes on a rampage. The Danube did that in the mid-nineteenth century, as attested by memorial tablets on old houses showing the height of the flood. The river Tisza all but wiped out Szeged in 1879, when it caused the death of hundreds and wrecked all but a few hundred houses. Since then the streams have been regulated. Yet the regulation has not accomplished its aim everywhere, as attested by raging floods in the east in 1970.

On the whole, however, nature has not been too unkind to Hungary. It is not in the path of such calamities as tornadoes, hurricanes or quakes.

3

These Are the People

WHAT KIND of people are the Hungarians? Are they blond or dark, short or tall? How do they compare with Americans?

In a typical American crowd, it would not be easy to pick out Americans of Hungarian descent. They do not have specific traits which distinguish their appearance. Being neighbors of Germans and Slavs, with whom they have intermarried for centuries, many of them are blond. Others have the dark coloring of the original Hungarians, who came from the East.

The average Hungarian at home is not as tall as the average American, but contemporary Americans are the tallest people in the world. As a rule, city-bred Hungarians are taller than their rural compatriots, perhaps because of a higher standard of living, with richer and more varied food.

Because of centuries of ethnic mixing, it is impossible to describe a "Hungarian type." That most typical Englishman, Leslie Howard, was Hungarian-born Arpad Steiner. He grew up in Pozsony, on the Danube, and was a young man when he went to London.

Three quarters of the Hungarian people are Catholics, and nearly all the rest are Protestants—Calvinists and Lutherans. Many Hungarians became Protestants during the Reformation, although the Counter-Reformation, under the energetic leadership of the Hapsburgs, won a majority of the people back to the Catholic faith. Protestants have dominated the Hungarian scene more intensely than their numbers justify. Several well-known statesmen, including the great Kossuth, have been Protestants.

At one time there was a sizeable Jewish population in Hungary. In the nineteenth century, many Jews considered Hungary a kind of "America" on the Danube. The country was then on the verge of great economic development, and some of its most important industries arose from the initiative of Hungarian Jews. The great metallurgical and steel works on the island of Csepel, for instance, are the work of Baron Manfred von Weiss. Hungarians of the Jewish faith built up much of the nation's impressive banking system, managed the best newspapers, and some of the best theaters. Ferenc Molnar, author of *Liliom,* became the best-known playwright in his country.

The German Nazis and their Hungarian henchmen murdered about half a million Hungarian Jews during World

War II. About one hundred and fifty thousand survived, and they continued to play an important part in the national life, particularly in the political and literary spheres.

For a small country, Hungary has made a remarkably large contribution to the arts and sciences. The Hungarian language has a strange word to denote a man of unusual gifts. The word is *langelme*—flaming mind. Hungary has produced a disproportionately large number of such flaming minds.

In arts, letters, and sciences many Hungarians have achieved worldwide fame. The "Hungarian rhapsodies" of Franz Liszt are perennial repertoire pieces, as are many of his piano compositions and symphonic poems. Bela Bartok, another immortal of music, is regarded as a leader of modern music. Fritz Reiner was the best known among the many famous Hungarian-born conductors. The name of Jozsef Szigeti, the violin virtuoso, stands out among the performing artists.

The best-known Hungarian lyrical poet of our century is Endre Ady, a harbinger of modern verse. The outstanding dramatist, Imre Madach, is known best for *The Tragedy of Man,* translated into many tongues. Among the contemporary Hungarian-born authors no name is better known than that of Arthur Koestler, whose novel, *Darkness at Noon,* about the "blood-purges" of the thirties in the Soviets, was hailed all over the western world, and whose penetrating analyses of our age have found an avid audience.

Best known among the plastic artists are Janos Fadrusz, the sculptor, Miklos Ybl, the leading architect, and, above all, Mihaly Munkacsy, historical and genre painter, several of whose works are exhibited in the United States. *Christ Before Pilate, The Music Room* and *The Pawnbroker's Shop* are among his most famous works.

Most people are familiar with the name of "the father of the hydrogen bomb," Dr. Edward Teller. In the same field, Dr. Leo Szilard launched America's nuclear age. The late Dr. John von Neumann, despite his premature death, became America's ranking mathematician. Theodore von Karman's work was essential to the design of contemporary airplanes. They all came from Hungary.

Hungarians distinguished themselves in many other fields, and particularly in the comprehension of the elusive nature of the soul of man. The best-known practitioner of "psychology in depth" was Dr. Franz Alexander, author of many important books, including the classic *Age of Unreason*. The work of Sandor Lorand, Geza Roheim, and Sandor Rado has helped to illuminate our exploration of the human mind.

The greatest honor that can be conferred on a scientist is the Nobel Prize, and Hungary has more than its share of prize-winners. Albert von Szent-Gyorgyi won the prize in medicine and psychology before World War II: George von Bekesy won it after the war. Georg von Hevesy won the Nobel Prize for chemistry in 1943. In 1963, Eugene Paul Wigner won it in physics for his "formulation of the symmetry principles governing the interaction of nuclear particles," even the title of which is difficult for a layman without a flaming mind!

The most highly coveted recognition in the world of sports is the Olympic Games, and here, too, Hungarians

A painting in the Hungarian National Gallery of the world-famous composer, Franz Liszt.

have been fabulously successful. At the games in Helsinki, in Melbourne, in Rome, and most recently in Tokyo, the Hungarians have been in the exalted company of the United States and the Soviet Union as winners of most of the medals.

One marked and consistent Hungarian trait is a love of freedom. Unfortunately, situated as they are on a main thoroughfare of the world, Hungarians have seldom had a full measure of freedom to enjoy. The courage and gallantry of the Hungarian "freedom fighters" of 1956 caused the world to take notice, but it is only the latest episode in a long history of rebellion against oppression.

There is one major difference between the Hungarians and their neighbors, and it is an important one. All the neighboring countries belong to one huge family, the Indo-European family of languages. Germanic, Slavic, Romance —all are Indo-European languages. Hungary is the only alien tongue.

Hungarian is a Finnish-Ugrian language. The Hungarians' nearest linguistic relations are the Finns, many hundreds of miles away, in the northernmost part of the continent. The Ugrians are footloose nomads in the frigid Arctic regions of Siberia.

Because Hungarian is basically different from the languages of neighboring countries, it is difficult for a Hungarian to learn his neighbor's tongue. Hungarian is an agglutinative language, the various parts of which are "glued" together. It has no prepositions nor auxiliary words. The following word illustrates its peculiar nature,

Legeslegmegengesztelhetetlenebbeknek.

This single word means "the most irreconcilable ones," and the word has a history:

Before World War I Hungary had access to a corner of the Adriatic Sea at the city and port of Fiume. (Today the city is called Rijeka and is in Yugoslavia.) Fiume formed then a separate part of Hungary in which most of the inhabitants spoke either Italian or Serbo-Croatian. An order came down from Budapest that applicants for government jobs in the city must master Hungarian. This was more than the local people could bear, and they scribbled that endlessly long word on walls to make two points: that Hungarian was an impossible language, and that the government was obstinate, or "irreconcilable."

In pre–World War I Hungary the ethnic minorities actually formed a majority, clustering mainly in the borderlands. They spoke a farrago of foreign tongues, mainly Slavic (Slovak, Slavonian, Croat, Serb), "Romance" (Rumanian and Italian), and German. After the First World War, the borderlands were joined to their adjacent homelands. Today only a small proportion of the non-Magyars live in Hungary, mainly Slovaks. On the other hand, millions of Hungarians have become "minorities" in the neighbors' lands.

Now that we have glanced at the land and at the people of Hungary, we shall look back over Hungary's history to see how the Hungarians have managed to maintain themselves in their fought-over corner of Europe. Surrounded by powerful nations, invaded by a succession of aggressive armies, speaking a language totally unrelated to those of their neighbors, where did the Hungarian people come from, and what forces shaped the Hungarians of today?

4

Out of the East

THE HISTORY of the Hungarians begins with a "riddle wrapped in a mystery inside an enigma," and the first chronicle of their history was written by an unknown monk. This first historian is pictured in a bronze statue in one of the city parks of Budapest, his features concealed in the cowl of his robe. No one knows his name, but scholars believe that he served King Bela III as a scribe, and that he died near the end of the twelfth century. His chronicle is entitled *Gesta Hungarorum,* or *Deeds of the Hungarians.*

Who are the Hungarians? They call themselves Magyars and their country *Magyarorszag,* or Magyarland. The word "Magyar" may be derived from the mythical Magor, brother of Hunor, reputed ancestor of the Huns. The brothers were sons of the giant Nimrod, described in the Bible as a "mighty hunter before God."

The Magyars came from Central Asia, we believe; they may have been descended from the nomads who rode to the West when Central Asia became a dust bowl. These nomads had possibly heard of the fertility of the West, of the wealth and magnificence of the great cities of Rome and Constantinople. They probably believed that the grass was forever green in the wonderful lands to the West.

The ancestral home of any nomadic people is hard to place, because they do not commit their memories to writing, and they do not build houses or cities which leave traces behind. Some scholars believe that the Magyars came originally from the Ural Mountains, which were within reach of grazing grounds as well as of the metal they used for tools. We do not really know much about them until they came West and made contact with more complicated civilizations.

As separate tribes the nomads were unsuccessful in war, so around 890 they drew up a compact between the tribes to act as one against enemies. Their grazing ground then was *Etelkoz*—Land Between the Rivers—in present-day Moldavia and Ukraine. It was good grazing ground, and it was crowded. Among the inhabitants were the Petchenegs, "blood-drinking beasts, carrion-eaters, unclean folk," who slaughtered prisoners instead of making them slaves. These wild people were in league with the Bulgarian Czar Simeon, who occupied a good part of the Balkan peninsula. In defense against these formidable foes, the Magyars allied themselves with the Byzantine emperor, Leo the Wise.

Even allied to the Eastern empire, the Magyars felt pushed from all sides. Under the leadership of Arpad, they decided to try their luck on the other side of the Carpathians. As they crossed the mountains on the Verecke Pass, they saw part of the land which was to be theirs for a thousand years. Hungarians call this episode *honfoglalas,* the "taking possession of the land." The time was A.D. 895.

Arpad's band of horsemen arrived in the land which was to be Hungary at exactly the right time. Charlemagne's great empire had collapsed. Prince Svatopluk, the Slav who had ruled over much of the Danubian region, had died in 894 and his holdings were breaking apart. The Magyars found only petty chieftains, whom they quickly subdued. They conquered the land of the mid-Danube in a remarkably short time.

The country they found seemed to answer their prayers. It had good soil which was not crowded with hungry people. It was a geographic unit wreathed on three sides by mountains. The mountains formed the walls of a gigantic natural fort which protected the invaders against further nomadic invasion. Toward the West, their country was open, and the gap in the mountains took them into Europe.

The easy conquest of the rich Danubian land whetted the Magyars' appetites. Their mountains sheltered them from the East, but they looked West and saw greener grass, watered by more abundant rains. In the land to the West, they saw a settled peasantry living in villages and towns. The Magyars decided to try their luck further.

Leaving a token force behind, the warriors departed in search of riches and glory. The Magyars were pagans who worshipped the forces of nature; they rode off to subdue the Christian West. They swept across Europe like a whirlwind. The civilized world, with little hope of effective resistance, regarded these savage barbarians with horror. A chronicler wrote: "Their stature is short, their behavior wild, and their tongue barbarous." The English word "ogre" may have been derived from the Byzantine name for Hungarian—*Ogor*. Frightened Westerners fell on their knees to pray: "From the Hungarians' wrath, deliver us, oh merciful God!"

The Hungarian warriors covered vast distances in an incredibly short time. Cutting across the European heartland, they crossed the lands settled by Bavarians, Thuringians, and Saxons, then reached the headwaters of their own Danube in the Black Forest. They crossed the Rhine and arrived in the area we call Alsace-Lorraine. There they feasted their greedy eyes on the fat lands of France.

Here the Magyars met resistance and were forced to veer southward, skirting the topmost regions of the Adriatic, spilling into the valley of the River Po. Lombardy, richest of all, could not hold them; they were determined to reach "Golden Rome." Rome was golden no more having been devastated by hordes of barbarian invaders, but the Magyars recalled the legends they had heard at home about the majestic city whose very streets were paved with precious stones.

The legends were believed by simple people, and the Magyars were simple as well as savage. They looted the land they crossed and sent the spoils to the distant Danube. While they never reached Rome, they plundered much of the Apennines peninsula. The famed British historian, Lord Macaulay, wrote: "The Hungarians, in whom the trembling monks fancied they recognized the Gog and Magog of prophecy, carried back the plunder of the cities of Lombardy to the depths of the Pannonian forests."

At first the Hungarians had the advantage of the initiative. Gradually the western leaders rallied their forces, collecting arms and men and building strong defenses. Otto the Great, an able ruler, occupied the throne of the Holy Roman Empire, and he was determined to wage a crusade against the Magyars. He wanted to build a new Rome, and he could not allow its peace to be disturbed by pagan invaders.

Otto took his stand against the Magyars at Lechfeld, near Augsburg, a Bavarian town on the Danube tributary Lech, in the year 955. Otto saw the battle as a great struggle between East and West, and he won a decisive victory. Badly defeated, the Magyars retired eastward to their home.

The Hungarians benefited greatly from their experience in the West. They had seen a settled peasantry and prosperous fields, hoed and harvested by well-fed men. They had seen, too, the impressive shrines in which the Westerners worshipped the Christian God.

The year 1000 was anticipated with foreboding. Many expected Judgment Day during that year; millions were filled with hope at the prospect of the Second Coming of Christ. Now the ruler of the Hungarians was Stephen—*Istvan*—Geza's son. Geza had been enthralled by the promise of Christianity and had embraced the Western creed—to him, the religion of success. Stephen took the final step,

The monument of St. Stephen on Fisher's Bastion in Budapest.

becoming a zealous missionary of the new creed among his people.

Stephen realized that the turbulent Magyars needed a strong central government. His subjects still followed tribal leaders and worshipped local deities. The Magyars were animists who believed that natural objects had each a soul, or as the Romans named it, *animus*. They feared and worshipped various natural forces and objects, including sun, wind, and such inscrutable objects as meteoric stones. It was difficult to please all of the gods, some of whom exacted the sacrifice of human lives. Rivalry among the gods matched the rivalry of the tribal leaders whose authority they were expected to protect. King Stephen proclaimed that there was only one God, the Divine Leader, who invested the king with his power. By the grace of God, the king was to rule over his land. Western prosperity appeared to reveal that one God could offer more to His followers than many competing gods; and if Hungary was to become as rich and strong as the Western nations, it must accept their God.

One great question remained: what branch of Christianity to join? In the West was the Catholic Church, with its seat in Rome; in the East, the Greek Orthodox Church with its seat in Constantinople. Differences in language and ritual separated the two, as well as politics and theology.

Hungary's neighbors to the east and south belonged to the creed of Constantinople, while those of the west and north had joined Rome. If Hungary followed Constantinople it would become an Eastern land; if Rome, it would become part of the West and of Europe.

King Stephen made an historic decision when he asked for Roman missionaries to convert his country. The Pope, Sylvester II, was so pleased by the request that he sent with the missionaries a royal crown, which forms the upper part of what came to be known as St. Stephen's Crown, or the "Holy Crown." Stephen was crowned on Christmas Day in the year 1000, and the crown was used by Hungarian rulers for many centuries. It became the symbol of supreme authority; indeed, a prince became the ruler of Hungary only after the holy crown had been placed on his head. (The crown is today in the hands of the United States. During World War II, when the United States and the Soviet Union were allies, Hungary's extreme right-wing government fled the Russians and handed the crown over to American authorities for safekeeping. It is still held in an undisclosed hiding place.)

What made King Stephen choose the Western church? First, he had a Western bride, a princess of Bavaria. He feared, too, that adoption of the Eastern creed would make his country a satellite of the Byzantine empire. Also, as we have seen, Hungary is open to the West and closed by mountains from the East.

Many of the Magyars considered the King's conversion a betrayal of the old order. Leading nobles rose against the ruler and tormented the missionaries: they put the Roman Bishop Gellert into a spiked barrel and rolled him into the Danube down the hill in Budapest which now bears his name. Nevertheless, most of Hungary was converted to Christianity.

Stephen turned to the West for his country's political organization as well as its religion. He divided the land into counties with royal stewards at their heads. The country was sparsely populated, and the fertile land needed farmers. The king encouraged immigration and exhorted

The statue of the martyred Bishop Gellert in Budapest.

his people to welcome the newcomers. When Stephen started his reign, Hungary was a tribal conglomerate; when he died, it was a country.

Stephen was canonized and became the patron saint of Hungary. His birthday, August 20th, was celebrated as a national holiday. In pre-Communist times a shriveled hand, reputedly Stephen's, was displayed in solemn procession through the old streets of Buda. A part of his skull is said to have been discovered recently on the Dalmatian coast of Yugoslavia, and so great is the fame of St. Stephen that Hungary's Communist government has begun negotiations with the Yugoslavian authorities to regain the precious relic.

St. Stephen was one of the Arpad dynasty. His successors lacked his authority, and when he died, the old nobles, now large landowners, sought to regain their power. Lacking a strong king, this was comparatively easy. Many of the estates were self-sufficient, the castles protected by sturdy walls. The local rulers had private armies, and they dispensed justice according to their whims. A weak king could do little to control them. The king, too, had a private army which could be used against the recalcitrant nobles, but he needed their money and their support. Even if he were willing to fight them, inadequate highways made them difficult to reach and strong defenses made a royal victory unlikely. The powerful chiefs were known as *kiskiralyok,* little kings.

A particularly weak king, Andrew II, occupied the throne at the beginning of the thirteenth century. The little kings took advantage of his weakness, joining against him to extort in 1222 the "Golden Bull." This became one of the most important documents in Hungarian history, a basic charter of the liberties of the subject—the noble subject, of course. The king promised not to tax the high nobility. The poor people, "ignoble" working folk, were to bear the burden of taxation. If the king waged war outside the country, he was to pay for it himself. If the king wished to quarter himself and his retinue in a nobleman's house, the consent of the host was needed. The ruler's sheriff could not detain a nobleman without a valid judgment of his noble peers. Finally, should the king violate any of the provisions of the Golden Bull, the nobility had the right to resist.

St. Stephen's work was undone. Hungary became the unhappy hunting ground of the little kings, and their rule could not be checked. A king could never be confident of his ability to summon an army to the country's defense. Just at this time, when Hungary was at its weakest, it was struck by one of history's greatest disasters.

5

The Ravenous Locusts

ONCE AGAIN, in the thirteenth century, horsemen appeared from the vastness of Asia. Perhaps a disastrous drought sent them in search of rich pasture and treasure in the West. These nomads were the Mongols, their name derived from the word "Mong" meaning brave in Chinese. They were also known as Tartars, and that word may be related to the Greek "Tartarus," meaning hell, for the Tartars brought hell to the nations they invaded.

Genghis Khan was the Mongol leader, and his grandson, Batu Khan, led the Mongol campaign into Europe. No force could stop these ruthless warriors, to whom the rich soil of the mid-Danube was irresistible. They scaled Hungary's protective mountain walls and descended into the plains. The decisive battle between Batu and the forces of Bela IV, the Hungarian king, took place at Muhi in 1241 between Buda and the northern mountain range. The Hungarian forces in their bulky armor were no match for the swift Mongol horsemen. Defeated, the Hungarian king mounted a fresh horse and raced away in a headlong flight through swamps, woods, and mountains. Finally, he found sanctuary on the Adriatic coast.

With Hungary's resistance broken, Batu Khan could have stormed into the West by way of the Danube. "From the wrath of the Mongols deliver us, oh merciful God!" prayed the priests and people of the West. Luckily for them, a son of Genghis Khan died far away in Asia. Batu turned around, leaving Hungary to its fate, and the rest of Europe was spared.

Even though the invaders were gone, Hungary was devastated. "The locusts are gone," the peasants wailed, "and so are our huts and crops." The impression of this awful period was so profound that the Hungarians coined an expression to describe disaster—*tatarjaras,* or Tartar invasion—which they continue to use today.

King Bela returned and set to work to rebuild his land. Again, there were not enough hands to gather the remaining grain, so he issued a call for immigrants. Peasants from abroad came in large numbers, taking possession of land whose owners had been killed. Magyars were replaced by new settlers of Germanic and Slavic origin.

The king encouraged the nobles to build or rebuild strong fortresses from which, hopefully, they could make a more successful stand in case of new invasions. With the king himself urging the little kings to strengthen their hold upon the country, his authority was weakened again. The Arpad dynasty had stopped producing great men, and the line died out with Andrew III, who died in 1301. Except for a short period, alien sovereigns were to rule in Magyarland for many centuries.

The little kings, who selected the new ruler, turned now to foreign dynasties. Theoretically, rulers were to be elected within the same dynasty, but this system became chaotic after the death of the last Arpad, for almost any relationship to a previous ruler was considered sufficient grounds for the election of an influential Prince. Thus, Hungarian rulers were to come from a wide variety of families: Bohemian, Bavarian, Austrian, Polish-Lithuanian, Luxemburger, and French. Laszlo IV of Hungary had a sister who married into the French house of Anjou. She became the mother of Charles Robert of Anjou, the first of that line to rule Hungary. In the time of the Anjou kings, Hungary was brought out of its Danubian isolation to become a major power with a role in world history.

During the Middle Ages, Hungary was one of the most important gold-producing countries of Europe. It was Charles Robert (Charles I of Hungary) who in 1325 had the first gold coins minted, encouraging saving as well as confidence in his financial integrity. Another Danubian country, Bohemia (now part of Czechoslovakia), supplemented the wealth of the region with abundant supplies of silver. Much of the silver was mined in the western mountains of Bohemia, especially in the "Valley of Joachim," known in German as Joachimsthal. In later years the coins of that valley came to be in great demand because of the quality of the metal and the honesty of the mint. The coin became known as Joachimnsthaler, abbreviated to "thaler," a word which crossed the Atlantic to become our "dollar."

Hungary flourished in the reigns of Charles Robert and his son, Louis the Great. They introduced many western administrative features, including a king's army stronger than those of the nobles. The large landowners had their own forces, *banderia,* which were subject to royal command in case of need. To protect the landowners (and their forces) from impoverishment, primogeniture was introduced. Under this system, inheritance of the bulk of the estate was limited to the oldest son. This strengthened the landowners' position and through them, the country's defenses, but it was eventually to encourage inefficiency and the persistence of outworn tradition.

A contemporary author, John Kukullei, wrote a chronicle of his period entitled *The Calm and Peace of the Age of Louis the Great.* He summarized the achievements of the famous king: "He left his country and its peoples in full possession of their liberties and customs, governing them with their own laws."

Hungary's good fortune was short-lived. A new danger arose in the East, and again the Magyar's land lay in the path of invasion. The Turks were on the move.

The Turks, too, originated in Central Asia. When the Mongols invaded their grazing grounds early in the thirteenth century, they were dislodged. Having lost their livelihood, they moved West and discovered that the once-mighty Byzantine empire was deteriorating. The Turks battered on the falling empire and acquired nearly all its land, with the exception of the strongly-defended city of Constantinople. They were forced to bypass the city, and they crossed the Straits and moved into the Balkan peninsula. Then they moved northward, toward the Danube which formed the boundary of Hungary. If the Turks could subdue Hungary, the road would be open to Vienna and the West.

The Turks were Muslims who looked on the Christians of the West as detestable infidels. They fought for their religion as well as for territory, and they had perfected a form of warfare which made them a formidable enemy. They were a nation in arms, professional fighting men, facing European amateurs who were called into service on a temporary basis. The Turks trained special troops whose only occupation was to wage war. These were called New Troops, *Yeni Sheri,* known to history as Janissaries. They were former Christians, kidnapped in war and brought up as warriors in the service of Islam. The Janissaries were educated to be anti-Christian fanatics.

In 1453 the Turks besieged the Byzantine capital, Constantinople, and captured it. It became the capital of their vast empire, situated on a main water thoroughfare between East and West. Centuries later, Napoleon said, "Whoever controls Constantinople can control all of Europe."

However, before capturing Constantinople the Turks had invaded Europe. The Hungarians rose to the challenge. Janos Hunyadi, whose name will live on, headed the Hungarian troops. Hunyadi was a great hero of a turbulent age, a great strategist, of great personal courage, a truly strong leader of strong men. Under his leadership, Hungary served as the Christian bulwark against the East.

Hunyadi replaced the feudal levies with a standing army of professional soldiers, instilling his men with holy zeal. The Western nations now changed their minds about the "abominable Hungarians"; they called them the Defenders of Christ, the Shield of Christianity, the Paladins of Faith.

The Hungarians stopped the Turks; not satisfied, the Hungarians recaptured much of the occupied territory. They regained a Balkan strong point, Sofia, which is today the capital of Bulgaria. Most of their successes were won

A monument of Hunyadi in Pecs. The church in the background was formerly a Turkish mosque.

in a series of battles known in history as the "Long Campaign of Janos Hunyadi."

The Turkish Sultan, Murad II, sued for peace, and a treaty was signed in 1444. Then international politics intervened. Envoys from the West persuaded Hunyadi that the Turks must not be allowed to recover their strength. The Hungarians protested that the treaty had already been signed, but the envoys replied that the Turks were enemies of humanity, and treaty or not, they must not be spared. The Pope himself assured the great commander that a pledge to the infidel Turk was not binding. Hunyadi resumed hostilities, and it seemed as if Heaven itself were punishing the breaking of the pledge. Hunyadi lost the war, and the Hungarian king lost his life.

Peace reigned for several years. Then Hunyadi recovered his strength, collected a large army, and attacked the Turkish strong point at Belgrade on the Danube. Belgrade was an important spot; if the Turks could maintain themselves there, they might later be able to move into Hungary and on to Vienna.

The decisive battle took place on July 21–22, 1456, and Hunyadi won. When the news reached Rome on August 6, the Pope declared that the day should be celebrated as the Feast of the Transfiguration, and so it is to this day. Hunyadi himself did not celebrate it. He fell ill of the plague and died in his camp. Few names shine as brightly in Hungarian history as that of the man whom his countrymen called *torokvero*—beater of the Turks.

6

A Just King and a Time of Troubles

THE NAME of Hunyadi was magic, and it was feared by Hungarian noblemen as well as Turks. After Hunyadi's death, intriguing little kings conspired with the weak King Laszlo V to put to death one of the sons of the great man, also named Laszlo. But another son did become Hungary's king, and he ruled for thirty-two years, 1458 to 1490.

The reign of this king, Matthias Corvinus, known as Matthias the Just, was a golden age in Hungarian history. The king was a beloved figure, and his deeds have been woven into legend. Matthias would have needed to reign several hundred years to be at all the places where he was seen by his eager subjects; according to one story, he disguised himself as a simple hunter and mingled with the common people, the better to know their problems and to serve them. In another typical saga, he turned up one day at a gamekeeper's hut, asking for lodging. The gamekeeper's beautiful daughter was dazzled by the beauty and courtesy of the stranger, and when he left, she and her father decided to visit him. They went to the address he gave them, and found that their guest's house was the royal palace, and he was their anointed king.

Matthias ruled during the Renaissance, an epoch of artistic and intellectual rejuvenation. He invited artists and scholars to his court and sponsored their work. He established a university at Pozsony, in western Hungary, and a theological seminary in Buda. He is remembered throughout the world for his magnificent collection of beautifully made books, known as the *Corvina*. The king maintained a special workshop for his books under Felix Ragusanus, a distinguished librarian who supervised the work of thirty

A sculpture of King Matthias the Just in the Hungarian National Gallery.

men. At its height, the collection contained three thousand volumes of exquisitely illuminated parchment bound in black and white velveteen. Even today, some of the surviving volumes are among the most valuable possessions of the great libraries of the world.

King Matthias established a professional fighting force, known as the Black Army from its specially designed black uniform. He anticipated the French Foreign Legion by inviting enterprising young men from other countries to join his force. His power kept the Turks in check, and he even conquered Vienna and other parts of the Hapsburg territory.

Matthias stood up against the "little kings" who might weaken his power. He strengthened the towns and their burghers, protecting the merchant middle class from the magnates' extortions. His best-remembered reform was his collection, codification and insistence on the laws of the land. The whim of the judge had no more power to make law; the judge must serve the law. This reform earned Matthias the name of "the Just."

At the end of his long reign, his people mourned him, saying, *"Meghalt Matyas kiraly, oda az igazsag,"*—"King Matthias is dead, and justice is dead with him."

Justice was dead, indeed. The Hungarian little kings chose a weak king, Wladislas II of the Polish-Lithuanian house of Jagiello. His reign marked the end of the beginning of freedom for the common people, and it is known as the Hungarian Time of Troubles.

The standing army of King Matthias was replaced by feudal levies, and the royal power slipped into the hands of the little kings. During Matthias' long check of the Turks in Europe, they had been strengthening their position at the opposite fringe of their realm, in Asia. Now they were ready to resume their march to the West.

The Christian world called for another crusade to stop the Turks. The bloody sword was carried around the country, in the traditional effort to make people join the army. Then something remarkable happened.

The response of the common people of Hungary was an ecstatic readiness to join the Crusade. The landowners began to realize that the holy war alone did not motivate the peasants. They left to escape from their masters, who treated them like beasts of burden. With the peasants gone, the fields were not tilled, and the landlords recognized a new danger.

The Hungarian noblemen acted in characteristic style. They rounded up the serfs ranged behind the crusaders' flag, put them in chains, and brought them back as if they had been fugitive slaves.

The leader of the crusaders was Gyorgy Dozsa, a Transylvanian nobleman with a distinguished record in the war against the Turks. Dozsa found his soldiers turning against their masters instead of their enemy, and he was sympathetic to their plight. He drew up a program of reform which was extremely radical for that day, curtailing the magnates' privileges and distributing some of their land among the landless serfs. The king's power was to be abridged, too, and that of the clergy, who made common cause with the nobility.

The landlords now tried to persuade the serfs who were

still away to come back, holding their families as hostages and subjecting their wives and children to torture. This treatment failed and the peasant crusaders became even more enraged. Their march was now marked by the blaze of burning manor houses, in which the landlords and their families were slaughtered. Once the crusaders started killing fellow-Christians, no power could stop them. The Turks, they said, could wait until they had wiped out the Hungarian nobility.

In the beginning the crusaders had the upper hand since the landlords had been taken by surprise. Before long, however, the nobility organized themselves and hired mercenary soldiers in Venice, Bohemia, and the empire. The mightiest of the noblemen, Janos Zapolya, was chosen to command the army. The magnates and their mercenaries, unlike the peasants, were well-armed, well-fed, and well-disciplined. The peasants were defeated, and retribution began.

Dozsa was captured, and his fate was torture and death. The peasants obviously could not all be put to death for they were needed in the fields, but punishment was imposed on them which was to endure for centuries. An assembly known as the "Savage Diet" met after the victory and enacted legislation known as the "Bloody Laws" which took from the peasants all the limited freedom they had known in the past.

For all practical purposes the Hungarian peasants became slaves, who could be bought and sold by their masters. They were subject to cruel and humiliating punishments, and the "twenty-five"—that many strokes of a whip —became a national institution. The peasants owed fifty-two days of unpaid work to their masters each year, and they owed the ninth and tenth part of their own produce to the noblemen and the church.

The distinction between noblemen and "ignoble" men who worked became more clearly marked than ever. According to the Savage Diet, God did not create men equal. On the contrary, it was blasphemy to assume that ignoble people were entitled to human treatment. The privileged classes were protected by laws, while the others remained beyond the reach of law or justice. *Misera plebs contribuens* was the Latin description of the peasants: miserable, tax-paying folk.

What of the Turks, meanwhile, who had witnessed the downfall of the great crusade? They took their time, planning the destruction not only of Hungary but of Western Christendom. Finally, in 1526, they crossed the Danube for their great drive to the West.

The Commander of the Turks was Suleiman, known in the West as the Magnificent. His own people called him *Kanuni,* the Lawgiver. Magnificent he was, and he gave laws to a vast empire which could be compared to the Roman Empire at the height of its glory. It extended from the Indian Ocean in the east to Algeria in the west, and its ruler could control the most boisterous warriors with a glance.

While Suleiman was strong, the king of Hungary was very weak. On the feeble shoulders of Louis II of the house of Jagiello rested the fate of the Western world. He ordered the bloody sword carried around the country again, but this time, the peasants were not allowed to join. The hastily assembled army had only twenty-six thousand soldiers, but the forces of Janos Zapolya were expected to fill its ranks.

The large army of Suleiman met the Hungarians at Mohacs, on August 29, 1526, on the bank of a small tributary of the Danube. The army of the Hungarian nobility rushed into battle, determined to knock out the enemy in the "first round." They took the Turks by surprise, and had Zapolya arrived on time, that might have been the end of the war. But he did not arrive, and the superior numbers and organization of the Turks began to show results. When the battle was at its height a sudden downpour turned the ground soggy and panicked some of the horses with thunder and lightning. The terrain turned into a bog, with still no sign of Zapolya. The king made an attempt to ford the stream, turned into a roaring river by a flash flood. The king's horse lost his footing; he fell. Several noblemen rushed to his rescue, but the king was drowned. This catastrophe further demoralized the Hungarians and emboldened the Turks, who now fell upon their enemy. The battle turned into a massacre while Zapolya loitered not far away. That gentleman had his eye on the throne and was not sorry to see the weak king lose a decisive battle.

Most of the Hungarian army perished, and in no more than two hours, the fate of the country was sealed. The Turks now had a way open up the Danube, to Vienna, and farther west. This turning point in history is known as the *Mohacsi Vesz*—the Mohacs Disaster.

The Turks' victory was so sudden and so complete that they suspected a trap and did not press their advantage. They tarried for some years before they pushed farther north and took Buda and Pest. Then, for a century and a half, the Turks ruled in Hungary. Only a sliver of the nation in the west and northwest remained to the Hungarians. Later the Turks tried to capture Vienna, but were turned back.

Hungary was now divided into three parts. The Turks ruled over most of the land, including the Great Plains between the Danube and the Tisza, and most of Transdanubia. They divided the land into administrative districts called *vilayets,* under their own pashas. They looted the country and kidnapped the sturdiest young men to serve as Janissaries. So many young Hungarians were taken that Magyar words could be heard all over the Turkish homeland.

The long Turkish reign has left a few marks on Hungary. A few minarets still stand, and Budapest has some baths constructed by the Turks. On the whole, though, the Turkish rule was singularly barren and devastating. No impressive monuments, works of art, or useful institutions were left behind. Nor did the presence of the Turks leave an appreciable influence on the ethnic composition of the population, since they did not intermarry with "infidel dogs."

Most of the words left by the Turks in the Hungarian language refer to extortion and banditry; some to agriculture. A few ruins, the old city of Eger and elsewhere, proclaim the Hungarian attempts to withstand the onslaught.

The sliver of western Hungary which had evaded the Turks now fell into the hands of the most powerful ruling family in the world—the Hapsburgs, who were to help the Hungarians oust the Turks, generations later, and to re-

The Matthias Church in Budapest.

place them as oppressors of the Magyars. The Hapsburgs ruled the western world from the Danube in the east to the Atlantic Ocean in the west, and beyond the ocean into newly-discovered America. "The sun never sets on the Hapsburg realm," people said, and muttered under their breath, "because God could not trust them in the dark."

The Hapsburgs, originally of Swiss-German stock, eventually became the rulers of Austria. Once established in Vienna, they commanded a strategic position and could extend their domain, gaining hold of Bohemia in the north, reaching out for Hungary. Elizabeth, daughter of Sigismund of Luxembourg, King of Hungary, married Albert of Hapsburg (ruled 1437–1439), and her marriage marked the beginning of the Hapsburg rule in Hungary. The dynasty was famous for its success in gaining territory through marriages.

Not only marriages assisted the Hapsburgs. For centuries, members of the family were elected as Holy Roman Emperors. Furthermore, theirs was the only strong dynasty in the midst of weak countries which were exhausted by an endless succession of wars. Hungary was one of these.

The third part of Hungary after Mohacs was Transylvania, the hilly, forested region in the east which had its own Princes from 1541 until 1711. Some of the Transylvanian Princes became important figures, for instance, Stephen Batory, who became a distinguished King of Poland. Francis Rakoczi II, the last of the Transylvanian Princes, was one of Hungary's great fighters for freedom. He fought the Hapsburgs, whose day of glory was now approaching.

7

Out the Turks and in the Hapsburgs

AT THE END of the seventeenth century, the Turks tried to penetrate into western Europe. They stormed the walls of Vienna, were rebuffed, and the defeat was fatal to their cause. The "irresistible force" was proved resistible. With amazing speed, Turkish power declined and the Turkish empire became "the sick man of Europe," kept alive, strangely, by the very powers the Turks had sought to destroy. The western nations feared that the collapse of Turkey would bring about a bloody struggle for power among themselves. The Russians, closest to the disintegrating empire, were particularly anxious to acquire its greatest asset, the Dardanelles. The waterway would have given them an outlet to the warm waters of the south, so badly needed for defense and trade,—the Czars' "warm water thirst."

The Hapsburgs were strong and Hungary was weak, as the Turkish power began to fall away. From 1526 on, Hapsburgs ruled over that part of Hungary which was not in Turkish hands. From the end of the seventeenth century, they ruled over all of Hungary. Their rule continued until the end of World War I.

Hungary was a wilderness after the Turks left; its farms neglected, its peasants living like animals. Epidemics ravaged the land, and the survival of an infant was a near-miracle. Sickness and starvation decimated the country, which seemed close to vanishing from the map.

The first duty of the Hapsburgs was to repopulate the deserted land. Settlers were invited, especially from German-speaking Europe—Swabians and Saxons, whose countries were overpopulated with a scarcity of arable land. Large groups of immigrants were settled in the Bacska and Banat regions of southern Hungary. As before, the nationality problems of Hungary were aggravated. The number of native Hungarians declined while the number of "foreigners" grew, which served the Hapsburgs very well. It was easier to rule over a nation that was divided into many nationalities, since one could be played against another.

The Hapsburg kings, Their Most Christian Majesties, had no intention of allowing the Hungarians to share in government. They were as oppressive as former rulers, and before long, Hungarian patriots were demanding freedom. Revolts flared up. Since the Turks were no longer a menace, some of the rebels made common cause with them against the Hapsburgs.

The most important revolt was led by Francis Rakoczi II, early in the eighteenth century. This dashing, romantic Transylvanian prince fought a strange war in which the Hungarians, calling themselves "Kurucok" or Crusaders, opposed Their Most Christian ruler, who was also the Holy Roman Emperor. The Hapsburgs were busy with another war in the west, and while it lasted, the Crusaders kept gaining ground. They occupied much of Hungary from the extreme north to the Danube.

A painting of the rebel Francis Rakoczi in the Museum of Fine Arts in Budapest.

Rakoczi won many battles but eventually lost the war. The Hapsburgs ended their campaign in the West and shifted their heavy forces to oppose the Prince. Rakoczi was defeated in 1711 and fled to sanctuary in Turkey. The Turks were friends of any enemy of the Hapsburgs. Rakoczi settled on the shores of the Sea of Marmora, living on as a perpetually romantic figure. Some stirring military marches celebrated his fame, including the immortal Rakoczi March of Hector Berlioz which was to accompany Hungarian soldiers against the Hapsburgs in years to come.

The Hapsburgs sat firmly in the saddle. While none of them earned the designation "Great," some were excellent monarchs. Maria Theresa (ruled 1740 to 1780) was one of these. She tried to make the Hungarians resign themselves to Hapsburg rule; she was good to them and they were loyal to her. The Hungarians thought so highly of the queen that they called her "King."

The "king's" neighbor, Frederick the Great of Prussia, tried to take by force the part of her kingdom known as Silesia. In those days, "Germany" consisted of some three hundred countries, large and small. Of these, Austria and Prussia were the largest, and they were rivals for leadership of the German states. Frederick, the Prussian, wanted to take Silesia from the Austrians.

Maria Theresa appealed to the Hungarian nobility for help, appearing before them with her infant child, Joseph, in her arms. The nobles exclaimed as one man, "Our life and blood for our king!" They offered lives and blood, but not money, and they marched off to war against the Prussians to lose yet another war. Frederick the Great took Silesia and attached it to Prussia, putting his country ahead in the race for domination of Germany.

Maria Theresa was grateful to her Hungarian subjects and helped them in various ways. She attached the city of Fiume, at the head of the Bay of Quarnero on the Adriatic Sea, to their country as a separate body, providing the access to the sea which they ardently desired.

The queen tried to improve the lot of the Hungarian peasants by limiting their obligation to their masters. She sought to open new markets for Hungarian farm products. Also, she attracted Hungarian noblemen to her Viennese Court, and some of their palaces still stand in the shadow of the *Hofburg,* the huge imperial residence. She established the *Theresianum,* an advanced school for youth of noble birth, including Hungarians.

Maria Theresa was succeeded by her son Joseph II (ruled 1780–1790), who, of the Hapsburgs, most nearly approached greatness. He wanted to help the common people and was called a "Jacobin," the designation of the most extreme French revolutionaries of that era. "All citizens must consider one another as brothers," he said, "and all distinctions among nations and religions must disappear."

He ordered that the serfs be emancipated, the Jews freed from the many restraints imposed upon them, and that discrimination against the Protestants should cease. He distributed food and medicine among the indigent, founded hospitals and orphanages, opened public gardens and parks. He also decreed that the nobility must share the burden of taxation with the common people.

Believing in a unified and centralized state, he concentrated the administration in Vienna and made German the official language of all his lands. More than seven thousand decrees and laws were issued in his name, evidence of the emperor's hard work for his people.

Joseph got no gratitude for his service. His enemies called him Anti-Christ, claiming that it was wicked to undermine the existing regime. Imperial decrees were disobeyed; the serfs were not freed; discrimination against minority religions continued. The peasants, influenced by their masters, turned against their well-meaning monarch. When the emperor's death was announced, church bells pealed in jubilation. Far ahead of his time, Joseph II died without recognition of his greatness.

After the French Revolution, and Napoleon's downfall in 1815 a new era of autocracy and tradition was ushered in. The Age of Metternich, taking its name from the archconservative Chancellor of Austria, was built on belief in the divine right of kings. It was Heaven's will that kings should rule and be obeyed, and ideas contrary to the system were godless and blasphemous.

Nevertheless, the idea that common people were human had spread even to Hungary. Educated men supported the heresy. One of them, Ignace Martinovics, was a Franciscan monk as well as a professor of mathematics and philosophy at the Monastic College of Buda. His Reformers' Association believed in the equality of man, a gross misinterpretation of the facts in the eyes of Metternich. Martinovics was secretly tried and publicly executed in the center of Buda, in a spot known thenceforth as Bloody Meadows.

Not even fear of the executioner could restrain the advance of political thought. The common people were too ignorant and downtrodden to help themselves, and it was members of the upper classes who led the advance. The reform movement received its greatest impetus from Count Stephen Szechenyi, a much-travelled and well-read nobleman. Returning from travels in the west, he was ashamed to look at his backward country where peasants lived like animals and landowners acted like God. Szechenyi led the opposition to Metternich in the Hungarian legislature.

Szechenyi believed that political progress could best be achieved by stimulating the economic, social, and intellectual life of the country. He wrote three books pointing the way to economic improvement through an imaginative policy of credit and investment. He advocated tax reform, and launched the Danubian Steam Navigation Company to help overcome his country's physical isolation. A wealthy man, he helped to found the Hungarian National Academy; its lovely building still stands on the Danube Embankment at Budapest.

Eventually, the Age of Metternich showed symptoms of decay. Old regimes toppled as a wave of reform swept over Europe. The revolutions of the 1830's began in Paris, spread to various parts of Italy and on to Poland, which was ruled by Austria, Prussia, and Russia.

New leaders arose in Hungary, men who believed that Szechenyi's approach was too slow, and that politics should take precedence over economics. They thought that economic conditions would improve automatically once Hungary was independent. The best representative of the "New

Man" was Lajos Kossuth (1802–1894), the great orator and statesman.

When Kossuth began his political career he was a dashing and handsome young man. He wore the full beard which became known as the "Kossuth beard." He rejected Szechenyi's go-slow policy, holding that the Metternich system would not relinquish its grip until it was forced to do so.

A statue of Kossuth in Szentes.

Kossuth prepared summaries of the proceedings of the Diet, stressing the points of the liberal members. The summaries were widely known and in great demand. The authorities forbade general distribution of his work; Kossuth disregarded the prohibition and was sentenced to four years in jail.

The prison was the fortress "Spielberg" on a hill in Bruenn, an infamous jail which would have crushed the spirit of a lesser man. Kossuth, however, benefited from his stay in prison, transforming his cell into a classroom. He learned English, studying the only books available to him— Shakespeare and the Bible—and mastered the language so well that he came to be considered the greatest English-speaking orator of his age.

Kossuth was released after three years, leaving with a degree of which he was proud: P.G., or Prison Graduate. The "degree" won him followers, because it was known that he had suffered for his liberal convictions. In 1847 he was elected a member of the National Diet, where he could command national attention.

In the following year, 1848, revolutions broke out all over Europe. The spirit of the age proclaimed that common people, too, had a natural right to live in dignity. Again, revolutions began in Paris and spread all over the continent, to the Poles, to the Italians, and to many German states. From Buda and Pest in the Hapsburg empire, the revolt spread to Vienna.

The emperor, Ferdinand V, was feebleminded; power belonged to Metternich and his clique. Kossuth, speaking for the revolutionary groups, demanded the abolition of feudal privileges and democracy for the entire country. When he spoke, he knew that a large number of Hungarians were behind him, and his fiery oratory enthralled the country. His proposed reforms included universal suffrage, equality before the law, trial by jury, governmental responsibility to the national legislature, a free press, a Hungarian national army, a national guard, a national bank, political amnesty for revolutionaries, equal taxation, and Hungary's reunion with Transylvania, separately administered by the Hapsburgs.

The revolt in Budapest spread to Vienna, where the people demanded an end to the oppressive regime of Metternich. The government was frightened, promised reforms, and forced the incompetent emperor to resign. He was succeeded by his nephew, Francis Joseph, then eighteen years old, who was destined to the longest reign in the history of his dynasty. Prince Metternich, too, was forced out of office, and his departure marked the end of the age which bears his name.

Hungarians were waiting eagerly for the expected reforms. Their greatest poet, Sandor Petofi, electrified his countrymen with his Appeal: *Talpra magyar Hiv a haza Itt az ido Most vagy soha* ("Arise, Hungarian; the Fatherland calls; the Time is now, now or never"). The Hungarians responded as did the French to the Marseillaise.

With the weak emperor gone, the forces of reaction at the Viennese court asserted themselves. They played on Hungary's weakness, its multitude of non-Hungarian nationalities. These they stirred up against the Hungarians, while they organized their military forces and marched against Hungary's strategic forts.

The Hungarians accepted the challenge. Kossuth had aroused the patriotism of the peasants, and a national army was organized. Previously, Kossuth had attempted to gain rights for Hungarians within the Hapsburg system; now he proclaimed that the "House of Austria, perjured in the sight of God and men, had forfeited the Hungarian throne." The Diet he called to Debrecen dethroned the Hapsburgs on April 19, 1849. Hungary became a republic, and Kossuth its "Governor."

Now that the lines were clearly drawn, Kossuth entrusted command of the Hungarian forces to a western-trained strategist, Arthur Gorgei. His army won many victories, including the reconquest of the twin cities of Buda and Pest. The Hapsburgs decided upon a desperate measure. With the Hungarians standing their ground successfully against the imperial forces and their own minorities, Vienna issued a call for help to Russia. The Czar, Nicholas I, believed that he had a holy mission to crush revolutions. To the Russian autocrat, the destruction of a democratic movement was a sacred duty.

The Russians came, led by Marshal Ivan Fedorovich Paskevich, a proven soldier. His forces, combined with those of the Hapsburgs, added up to a total of 370,000 men against 180,000 Hungarians. The latter, poorly armed, fought like fanatics, but were crushed by the superior manpower of the enemy. The decisive battle was lost by the Hungarians near the town of Vilagos on August 13, 1849. "Hungary lies at your Majesty's feet," Paskevich informed the Czar.

The victors were far from merciful. Drumhead courts sentenced many of the revolutionaries to be hanged, or in cases of leniency, shot. The Hungarian revolution, which had won the admiration of the world, ended in disaster.

The Hapsburgs had won, but their victory would be short-lived. When they called in the Czar, the whole world had seen their weakness. Another long-range result of the war was the hatred conceived then by the Hungarians for Russia and the Russians. It was to break out a century later in a new and violent form.

Kossuth avoided capture and made his way to Turkey, which was still a friend to anti-Hapsburgs. He was interned at Vidin, at Shumla, and at Kutahia, being moved around because of rumors to the effect that the Viennese government planned to kidnap him.

Kossuth had won worldwide fame, and he received invitations to visit several countries. He accepted an invitation from the United States, and the American man-of-war *Mississippi* called for him in September, 1851. He stopped off in Britain, where Richard Cobden wrote of him: "He is most certainly a phenomenon. Not only is he the first orator of the age, but he combines the rare attributes of a first-rate administrator, high moral qualities, and unswerving courage."

The Hungarian leader's welcome in America had few precedents. Charles Sumner, the anti-slavery champion, recalled: "I remember Kossuth's landing. The admiration, the enthusiasm, and the love of the people which had been gathering force across the Atlantic, gave him an ovation which only two men had ever received—Washington and

Lafayette." The welcome in New York was ecstatic.

Dozens of books and poems were written in honor of the statesman. James Ford Rhodes, an American scholar, called the 1850's "The Age of Kossuth." Today, there are Kossuth Streets, Kossuth Avenues, and Kossuth monuments in many American cities.

At the end of his triumphant trip, the great man returned to Europe and settled in Turin, in northern Italy. He was in his nineties when he died, his name linked with those of all the great freedom fighters of history.

8

An Agreement and
New Problems

AFTER Vilagos, Hungary became an Austrian colony. The counties, former bulwarks of local self-government, were replaced by districts ruled from Vienna. German-speaking officials administered Hungary in a centralized system headed by the crown minister Alexander Bach, who returned to many features of the odious old regime. Yet he could not turn the clock back. The serfs remained free, and several other reforms stayed in force.

However, the weakness of the Hapsburg empire became more apparent every year. The Austrians lost prosperous parts of northern Italy which they had held since the downfall of Napoleon. Even more humiliating was the defeat they suffered at the hands of the Prussians in the Seven

Weeks' War of 1866, which called for new diplomacy.

Advisors of the emperor, fearing another rebellion, believed that the time had come to reach an agreement with the Hungarians. Some thoughtful Hungarians shared this view, including the statesman Ferenc Deak, who wrote an article about the problem in an influential daily newspaper. It was published on Easter Sunday and became known as the "Easter Article." Deak expressed the belief that the deadlock was hurting Austrians and Hungarians alike, and he proposed a compromise. The Hungarians were to have a free country, but the emperor of Austria should be the Hungarian king. In matters of common interest (foreign affairs, defense, and the finances relating to them), policy should be made and executed jointly.

Finally the conflict was resolved on the basis of the Easter Article, and the Compromise (*Ausgleich,* in German) of 1867 was reached. The Compromise transformed the country into a Dual Monarchy of two equal partners. The ruler of the two countries was one person, Emperor of Austria and King of Hungary. Budapest became a separate capital of a separate kingdom.

Under the Compromise, Hungary was to have its own government with legislative, executive, and judiciary branches. The Hungarians built one of Europe's most magnificent parliamentary buildings to house their legislature, a beautiful Gothic edifice on the Danube. The two countries established a joint administration for foreign affairs, defense, and related finances. The imperial government was transformed into the imperial and royal administration, *kaiserlich und koeniglich,* often abbreviated as k.u.k., the trademark of the Dual Monarchy.

The solution was welcomed by Austrians and Hungarians alike, and Ferenc Deak was titled *haza bolcse,* the sage of the fatherland.

The agreement did not, of course, eradicate all the problems of the two nations. On paper the two countries were equal, but really Austria was more equal than Hungary. It was richer, more populous, and much more industrialized. With three-fifths of the population of the Monarchy, Austria was more influential in foreign affairs, and therefore in defense.

One of the most notable Hungarian statesmen of the Dual Monarchy was Count Julius Andrassy, Sr. The French knew him as *le beau pendu*—the handsome hanged man. He had fought the Hapsburgs in 1848 and was sentenced to death by their court. He was hanged, too, but only in effigy because he had fled abroad. Subsequently, he made his peace with the Hapsburgs and was granted a pardon. He returned to Hungary and became the country's first Prime Minister after the Compromise. Later—in the seventies—he served as the entire Monarchy's Minister of Foreign Affairs and played a leading role at the Berlin Congress of 1878, where many European problems were settled. Now the Hapsburgs had every reason to be thankful that Andrassy had managed to keep alive, in spite of the sentence of death.

In the course of time, many Hungarians became dissatisfied with the Compromise. They wanted more say in the conduct of foreign affairs, and they wanted the Hungarian language used in Magyar regiments. This controversy set the tone of Hungarian politics until 1914, with those who were satisfied with the Compromise known as the "67ers," and those who were dissatisfied, the "48ers."

Meanwhile the problem of the Hungarian minorities continued to plague the country. These groups, descendants of the immigrants called into Hungary after the devastation wrought in turn by Tartars, Turks, Hapsburgs, and Russians, spoke their own languages and kept to their own communities. The Slovaks, Croats, Slovenes, Serbians, Rumanians, Italians, Swabians, and Saxons who made up the "minorities" of Hungary were probably a real majority as compared with the Magyars. Before the Compromise, the Hapsburgs had favored them; after the Compromise, they

Parliament Building in Budapest, built to house the legislature established in 1867.

met harsh treatment from the Hungarians. They lacked public schools, could not cultivate their own languages and culture, and had little opportunity to present their grievances in the national parliament.

The Hungarians had achieved almost complete independence for themselves, and they valued it highly. They were not willing, however, to allow even a hope of independence or cultural survival to the Hungarian minorities. Furthermore, Hungarian statesmen did everything they could to block the progress of the small nationality groups within the Hapsburg empire outside of Hungary.

The economic changes worked by the Compromise were generally favorable. The Hungarians were no longer at the mercy of Austria in questions of tariffs. They installed industrial plants, processing native farm products as well as heavy machinery. With the help of government benefits, some fifteen hundred new industries were founded within one decade. Large new banks were formed, and Budapest became a major financial center. The railways were extended and improved; fares were reduced. School attendance was made compulsory; sanitation was improved; attempts were made to raise farm productivity. Tourists discovered Budapest, and it became one of the gayest cities in Europe, with gypsy music, excellent wine, beautiful women, brilliant concerts, and theater.

Much of this improvement benefited only the top layer of Hungarian society. Millions of peasants had still to struggle along with little or no land while huge tracts belonged to a few magnates. The plight of the landless farm worker was particularly sad. One of their spokesmen,

Sandor Csizmadia, presented this gloomy picture at the turn of the century: "I have watched the life of the peasants on the estates, three or four families, sometimes as many as twenty to twenty-five persons living in the single room of a hut. I have seen men collapsing of famine on the richest soil of the country, and I have also seen men being virtually drowned in their fat. Families of the *puszta* are working for fifteen *krajcars* (a dime) from three in the morning till ten at night."

The working day of the factory hand was very long, too, and he earned not much more than the farm worker. When the labor unions began to agitate for an eight-hour day, they met violent opposition.

Hunger typhus was endemic in parts of the country, and tuberculosis was called the Hungarian malady. Pellagra and other vitamin-deficiency diseases sapped the people's health. In some areas, half the infants died before the age of five. Iniquitous tax assessments favored the rich; the richer the taxpayer, the less his share of the burden.

The poor had two ways of protecting themselves. Many left the country as emigrants, most of these to the United States. A single villager who took passage to America, got a job in a coal mine and made his fortune (sometimes as much as ten dollars a week), sent for his family. News of his success spread to the neighbors. Families scraped together the steamship fare for one "pioneer"; once in America, he helped his relatives to join him. In one peak year, 1907, nearly two hundred thousand people left Hungary for America. About a million people, representing fully 5 per cent of the population, left Hungary before the First

World War. Hungarians began to worry about "race suicide."

There was another means of race suicide. Families decided to have no children, or only one. This trend became known as the *egyke* system. *Egy* means "one" in Hungarian, and *ke* is a diminutive; hence, "one little one."

The lower classes had no voice in government; the beautiful parliament building was filled with landlords, industrial tycoons, and financiers. Suffrage was not universal and seldom secret, for the strangest reasons. "The Hungarian is so honest," said one Prime Minister, "that he does not want to vote in secret."

The most important political leader of the era was Count Stephen Tisza, several times Prime Minister. Tisza was convinced that only the upper classes could rule, that little people had little thoughts and could not tackle the vast problems of politics. He totally disregarded the interests of the common man. The great hopes of the inspired leaders of the past—Szechenyi, Kossuth, Deak—had failed to materialize.

The Hungarian leaders, failing to keep up with their changing times, were not able to foresee the volcanic forces which were to wreck the foundations of their system. Their inordinate power, and that of fellow-statesmen in many nations, came to grief in the cataclysmic twentieth century.

9

Two Great Wars

On June 28, 1914, the Archduke Franz Ferdinand—heir to the Austro-Hungarian throne—was assassinated in Sarajevo. His murderer was a young Serb who wanted to draw attention to the fate of millions of Slavs who lived under the rule of the alien Hapsburg empire.

Austria accused the Serbian government of condoning the murder, and delivered an ultimatum so unjust and so severe in its demands that Serbia could not fulfill its terms. The military clique in Vienna sought a quick victory against a weak neighbor to strengthen Austria's position in the tightly-drawn European balance of power. The war party believed that war could be confined to Austria and Serbia. They were totally mistaken; once set in motion, no diplomatic efforts could contain the conflict. By the end of the summer, almost all of Europe was at war.

Hungary, Austria, and Germany were allied and were known as the Central Powers. The strongest nation in that group was imperial Germany; it was eventually joined by the Ottoman Empire and the Kingdom of Bulgaria. The Central Powers faced the Triple Entente of Britain, France, and Russia, joined later by Italy. In 1917, the United States entered the war on the side of the Entente.

The German Emperor, William II, predicted that his victorious armies would be home before the autumn leaves fell. The war lasted more than four years, taking a hitherto-inconceivable toll of men and nations.

The Dual Monarchy fought on two fronts, against the Russians and the Italians. It fought with the weary army of a worn-out monarchy in a weird new form of warfare which neither generals nor statesmen could understand or control.

Because of the devastating effect of new weapons, the soldiers were forced to burrow into trenches, living almost underground. On the western front the two armies were almost evenly matched, locked in a death grip in the muddy fields of northern France. As both armies were sinking to critical weakness, the United States and its huge resources turned the tide for the Entente. On November 11, 1918, the Central Powers were finally defeated.

The Dual Monarchy of Austria-Hungary disintegrated even before the end of the war; the worst fears of the pre-war leaders came true after the defeat. The Czechs of Austria joined with the Slovaks of Hungary to set up their own country, Czechoslovakia. The Austrian Poles, with their brothers in Germany and Russia, established the Polish Republic. The Rumanians of eastern Hungary made common cause with the Rumanians across the mountains, and a Greater Rumania came to life. The South Slavs of Austria and Hungary joined the kingdom of Serbia in a new nation, Yugoslavia. The Italians of the Dual Monarchy were united with the kingdom of Italy.

During the war, in 1916, Francis Joseph died. He was succeeded by the timid young king Charles IV of Hungary, Charles I of Austria, who lost both of his thrones and was forced into exile. He was the last ruling monarch of the ancient dynasty.

All the losers paid a terrible price, none more than the Hungarians. They lost 71 per cent of their pre-war territory, and 60 per cent of their pre-war population. Millions of Hungarians became the subjects of victorious neighbors. Hungary lost 61 per cent of its arable land, 88 per cent of its timber, and 56 per cent of its industrial plants.

In its thousand-year history, Hungary had been afflicted by numberless adversities. Devastated by Turks and Tartars, oppressed by Hapsburgs, invaded by Russians, she had retained at least her mountain frontiers. Now that magnificent protection was gone; Hungary was stripped of her natural frontiers as well as her richest land.

The Hungarians swore that they would never resign themselves to their fate. Children continued to study their nation's history, and their maps continued to show the historical frontiers. The lost regions were marked "Under temporary occupation."

The Hungarians brought their misfortunes to the attention of the world in one of the most successful publicity campaigns of recent times. The world became acquainted with a few words of the difficult Hungarian language: *Nem, nem, soha*—no, no, never—the cry of the Hungarians. Prayerfully, the children intoned:

> I believe in one God
> I believe in one Fatherland,
> I believe in Hungary's resurrection.

Several regimes followed the Great War in quick succession. After King Charles' departure, a republic was established under the leadership of Count Michael Karolyi. Karolyi was one of the richest men in the land, an aristocrat with liberal views. One of his first programs was the distribution of his vast estates among the peasantry. He did not remain in power for long; with the country being dismembered, more extreme views prevailed.

In the spring of 1919, a group of extremists seized power. They were led by Bela Kun, a Communist who tried to copy the Russian Bolsheviks. He formed a government which disintegrated in a few months, lacking any idea of how to run a country. That same summer, the Communists were supplanted by a regime of the opposite extreme, White Terror following Red. The new government was headed by Nicholas Horthy de Nagybanya, former commander of the Austro-Hungarian navy, now "Regent of Hungary."

Nominally, Hungary was still a kingdom, but when King Charles tried to regain his throne Horthy had him deported by the British to an island in the Azores. The new regime set up detention camps for its enemies. It was not only anti-

Communist but anti-Socialist, anti-Semitic, and anti-demo-
cratic. The country was ruled by large landowners, with
their followers in the "gentry," and by great industrialists,
with the army and the clergy in the background. Horthy
himself was not very intelligent, and he was little more than
a figurehead for these powerful men.

The rigors of the Horthy government were tempered
eventually and particularly during the 1920's when Count
Stephen Bethlen was Premier. Bethlen had help from the
League of Nations in his attempts to stabilize Hungary's
finances. A Boston lawyer, Jeremiah Smith, Jr. was the
League's High Commissioner in Hungary, and he did a
great deal to put the country back on its feet. American
bank loans were secured, and the national budget stabi-
lized. Jeremiah Smith was hailed as Hungary's benefactor,
and a statue was erected in his honor in Budapest.

Neither Smith nor the League could avert the economic
depression which struck most of Central Europe in the
wake of the collapse of the New York Stock Exchange in
1929. The bad years hit Germany especially hard, bring-
ing large-scale unemployment and dissatisfaction, and producing a climate in which a maniac could proclaim himself a messiah. Adolf Hitler, during the thirties, organized
his New Order for Germany and her neighbors. In Hitler's
plan, Hungary was to supply the Reich with raw materials
and food.

By this time Bethlen was gone, and the Hungarian government was headed by Julius Gombos, leader of the
Party of National Unity and an admirer of Hitler. He saw
the New Order as "the wave of the future." Gombos was

not the only Hungarian to admire Hitler; there were others, including Bela Imredy, head of the Party of Magyar Life. Hitler was obsessed with hatred of the Jews, and he demanded that his satellite nations should pass anti-Semitic laws.

In collaboration with Benito Mussolini, the Italian dictator, Hitler began to rearrange the map of Europe. They returned southern Slovakia and northern Rumanian Transylvania to Hungary. Then Hitler incorporated Austria into Greater Germany. Successful so far, he demanded that the German-speaking peoples of the Czech border areas

A typical servants' house on a large estate before 1945.

should be attached to his Third Reich. He won the agreement of the western democracies to his accomplishments at the famous Munich conference in the autumn of 1938, where he announced that he had made his last territorial demand.

Before many months went by, Hitler had gone back on his word and made the Czech part of Czechoslovakia a "protectorate" of his own and the Slovak portion his satellite. His next territorial claim, in Poland, ran headlong into that nation's mutual-assistance pacts with Britain and France. When Hitler's armies marched into Poland, France and Britain declared war.

Before he entered Poland in the late summer of 1939, Hitler had concluded a non-aggression pact with the Soviet Union. He spent almost a year digesting the bulk of Poland (Russia took care of the rest), then turned West in 1940. His "blitzkrieg" overwhelmed France, and the British expeditionary forces had to be evacuated from the continent. France was occupied, but Britain stood firm, at first alone, later as the center of resistance to the German dictator.

After one more year, Hitler turned against the Russians, and at this point he called on the Hungarians to join his forces. The Hungarians were not eager to do so, realizing that his early victories might not continue. Hitler, to force Hungary into war, had some of his planes marked with Soviet markings. These planes bombed Hungarian towns, and Hungary declared war on Russia.

The Germans swept deep into Russia, all the way to the Volga River. There, at Stalingrad, in the great turning point of the war, the hunter became the hunted as the Russians defeated the German army and pushed them west. During this retreat, Hungarian forces were employed near the river Don in the vicinity of Voronezh. In the first months of 1943, nearly the entire Hungarian Second Army was lost—forty thousand soldiers killed, eighty thousand captured. For all practical purposes, Hungary was out of the war.

America had entered the war in December, 1941, and by 1943, the Grand Alliance was clearly on its way to victory. The Hungarians realized that Hitler was going to lose the war, and Horthy tried to conclude a separate peace. On October 15, 1944, he issued a proclamation of armistice which he could not back up with force. Hitler had him arrested and removed from Hungary.

The government in Budapest was turned over to one of Hitler's local adherents, the half-mad Ferenc Szalasi, leader of an extremist organization called the "Arrow Cross." Szalasi believed that there were three dominant forces in the world: Hungarianism, Marxism, and Christianity. He intended to wipe out Marxism and transform Christianity to serve his ends. Hungary was to lead a "Carpathian Danubian Great Fatherland," following a program of the "trinity of the soil, blood, and work." None of this made any sense to sensible men.

By the end of 1944 the Russians were approaching Budapest. Instead of concentrating their energies on resistance, the Arrow Cross lined up their presumed enemies, mostly Jewish Hungarians, on the Danube Embankment and machine-gunned men, women, and children into the river.

The Russians raced into Pest and occupied that portion of the capital in mid-January, 1945. The Germans eluded them for a while by racing across the Danube and blowing up its bridges. The Russians were halted on the Embankment but not north of the capital, where they crossed the river and turned back on Buda.

Then the German radios began to crackle, presumably with a message from the High Command. It gave orders for its soldiers to break out on a broad avenue between two hills in Buda. As they did so, Russian machine guns fired and the German soldiers were slaughtered. They had been led into a trap and were completely defeated.

The Hungarian Arrow Cross kept one step ahead of the Russians, marching westward across Transdanubia and slaughtering its opponents along the way. Eventually, most of its members found their way to Germany, where many of them have settled.

The Soviets were now masters of the broad belt of land from the Baltic to the Adriatic. They dominated the governments of the Eastern European countries. Hungary became an integral and essential part of the long, Russian-dominated frontier.

10

Hungary Since 1945

WHEN THE Soviets took control of Hungary in 1945, they set up a coalition government of several parties, the most important of which was the Small Landholders. A Communist, Matthias Rakosi, became the key person in the government, and his name is associated with the decade that followed.

A dedicated Communist, Rakosi had played a part in the short-lived Hungarian Bolshevik regime after World War I. He had escaped the White Terror, returned to work underground, been captured and spent many years in jail. After the non-aggression pact was signed between Germany and the Soviet Union, an era of good feeling prevailed and Horthy pardoned Rakosi, who returned to Russia. Rakosi spoke Russian fluently, married a Russian, was ruthless, unscrupulous, and an indefatigable worker as well as a man of great intelligence.

When the Hungarian Provisional Assembly met in Debrecen after the war, Rakosi was active behind the scenes. At that meeting, the damage suffered during the war was estimated and measures for reconstruction were passed. Hungary had lost 90 per cent of her bridges, 89 per cent of her rolling stock, and 69 per cent of her locomotives. The country was almost paralyzed.

Disregarding these losses, Moscow exacted a heavy tribute from the Hungarians, mostly in services and goods. Soviet-Hungarian companies were formed in which the Russians played the dominant part. The people of Budapest, with tongue in cheek, said, "The Soviet-Hungarian Danubian Navigation Company is engaged in a truly fifty-fifty enterprise. The Hungarians have the right to navigate the river sidewise, the Soviets lengthwise."

In the national elections after the war, the Small Landholders, a center party, polled a majority of votes in spite of help extended to the Hungarian Communists by the Russians. The Communists received only 17 per cent of the vote; the Small Landholders, 56 per cent. The Social Democrats and the National Peasants' Party took the rest of the seats in parliament. The Prime Minister, Ferenc Nagy, was a member of the Small Landholders, but his authority was sharply curtailed by Rakosi's power.

The victorious Allies met in Paris in 1946 to settle the fate of their former smaller enemies, including Hungary. The national boundaries remained at the limits fixed after the First World War, and Hungary lost a small additional territory across the Danube to Czechoslovakia.

In 1948, an event occurred which shocked the Communist world. Yugoslavia's Communist Marshal Tito was expelled from the fold for "nationalistic deviation." He asserted that he was a Communist, but not of the Russian brand. It was made perfectly clear by his expulsion that Moscow expected its comrades in every country to toe the party line. Stalin felt that Tito's "nationalist heresy" might be imitated in other countries, and he instructed Rakosi to put an end to the coalition government of Hungary and to assume full power.

Ferenc Nagy was deprived of his post, and Rakosi called new elections. His party was given a new name—the Hungarian Working People's Party. Only "safe" citizens were allowed to vote, and Hungary became a fully Communist country.

The Hungarian currency, the *pengo,* had begun to lose value during the war; after the war, devaluation progressed at a fantastic rate. It lost its value until one American nickel was worth four hundred thousand *quadrillion* pengos, an inconceivable figure. Suddenly, the decline was stopped and a new unit of currency, the *forint,* was introduced.

Under the Rakosi regime, a Soviet system of planned economy was installed in Hungary. As in Russia, the accent was on heavy industry, and heavy machinery had to take precedence over consumer goods. Rakosi realized that if Communism was to survive it would have to raise the standard of living, but he knew, too, that the people would have to make sacrifices, to work hard and live on short rations, during the first years of the regime. Once the machines had been built and installed, more attention could be given to food, clothing, and shelter.

Roads had to be repaired and new ones built. Many country people lived in straw-thatched mud huts, which had to be replaced by more durable houses covered with tile.

The worst injustices of the old regime had been inflicted on rural Hungary. Some of the great landowners had incredibly vast estates, tens of thousands or even hundreds of thousands of acres belonging to one family. The Communist government broke up these estates and distributed the land among the peasants—but not for long. Rakosi wanted to show the people that small parcels of land were inefficient. Pressure was applied on the peasants to enter collectives, patterned on the Soviet *kolkhoz*. These were large units in which efficient agricultural methods could be employed, with common ownership of farm machinery. The government introduced fertilizers, improved seed, new farm machinery, and farm products; it undertook large-scale irrigation, drainage, and marketing.

The peasants, who were forced to join the collectives, were unhappy. They preferred to own their own land, even if it meant continued poverty and inefficiency.

The factories, too, introduced a strict regime of speed-up operations, in an effort to bring nearer the brightly planned future. A vast propaganda campaign was initiated, called "education," to show the Hungarians that they were better off than ever before. Workers had to spend long hours at lectures and meetings, listening to the repetitive mes-

Budapest, 1957. The rubble is cleared away after the uprising.

sages of the state. And the messages were boring.

Grumbling began, but grumblers got short shrift. Rakosi was served by a terroristic secret police, the AVO, or "state defense organization." Careless words brought a midnight knock on the door; even true Communists were not safe from the terror. The accusation of "Titoism" was enough to subject a man to torture and jail. Barbed wire, lookout towers, and trip-mines moved into Hungary and separated her from the West.

In March, 1953, an epoch ended with the death of Stalin. In Hungary, Rakosi even had to resign for a time; he was succeeded by Imre Nagy, who had once been accused of the Titoist heresy. (Imre Nagy is not to be confused with Ferenc Nagy, the ousted Premier.) Rakosi still held on, however, operating behind the scenes and eventually replacing Nagy with his comrade Erno Gero.

In the summer of 1956, another dramatic event occurred in Eastern Europe, this time in an industrial city of Poland, Poznan. The Poles, traditionally liberty-loving, insisted that the Soviet hold on their country must be loosened and that their Stalinist leaders must be replaced by the man they preferred, Wladislaw Gomulka. Gomulka was a Communist, but he appeared to be more moderate and less of a Kremlin slave than the men in power. Shots rang out; several people were killed; the Soviets yielded. Gomulka became Poland's No. 1 man.

Poles and Hungarians have a great deal in common. They are near-neighbors, and both peoples have stood their ground for centuries against aggression. Both nations are intensely nationalistic. The Hungarians observed the developments in Poland with fervent interest, and many of them decided that their opportunity for action had come.

Action began on the evening of October 22, 1956. A group of dissidents (mainly college students) held a meeting in Budapest at which they voiced their demand for a freer Hungary. They wanted freedom of speech, free general elections, a new government headed by Imre Nagy, the removal and trial of the Hungarian Stalinists, and the withdrawal of Soviet troops.

The crowd wanted to broadcast its demands, and it began to move toward the Radio Building in the center of

Budapest. Members of the hated AVO (secret police) were stationed around that building, and they shut the gate in the face of the crowd. Tumult and confusion ensued, and tear gas bombs were thrown by the police from the upper floors of the building. The crowd became excited, the noise became tremendous, and a shot rang out. Who fired it? Because of the excitement and confusion, no one knows, but it marked the beginning of the historic Hungarian uprising.

The crowd turned on the AVO men, some of whom were tortured and lynched on the spot. The students were joined by other citizens, and factory workers from the industrial sections of nearby Csepel and Ujpest started moving on the capital. When a statue of Stalin in Budapest City Park was knocked from its pedestal, the uprising was in full swing. Many members of the Hungarian armed forces, and even of the police, joined the rebels.

Revolutionary action began, too, in other industrial centers, especially in Gyor, Miskolc, and Pecs. The Gero government fell, and Imre Nagy took over as Premier. An heroic wartime underground fighter, an anti-Communist, Joseph Kovago, became the Lord Mayor of Budapest.

Rakosi's regime disintegrated overnight and he and his henchman, Gero, vanished from sight. The peasants abandoned the collectives; the railway workers proclaimed a strike; the political police were dissolved. Premier Nagy declared that new elections would be held and he supported Pal Maleter, former deputy minister of defense, who was organizing the uprising. Nagy himself officially went over to the insurgents; then he took a momentous step. He proclaimed that Hungary was leaving the Soviet bloc, becoming a neutral nation. He appealed to the West and to the Soviet Union to be guarantors of Hungarian neutrality.

The Russians hesitated. They did not want to tarnish the favorable image of the "thaw," that had followed Stalin's death, but they could not allow Hungarian independence to endanger their position in Eastern Europe. After a few days of indecision, a large mechanized force was assembled. Twenty-five hundred Russian tanks, with thousands of supporting vehicles, got under way to Hungary. They immediately began to take over strategic points: airways, railway centers, military installations, and trunk roads. Soviet forces swept into Budapest, where they faced street battles of the utmost ferocity. Nagy announced that he was remaining at his post, and that his troops were in combat with the Soviets.

As the Russians advanced upon the center of Budapest, the insurgents threw up barricades to retard the advancing tanks. They were equipped only with light arms and "Molotov cocktails"; they could not halt the Soviets, nor could they hold them in the other Hungarian cities. As they fought, they appealed to the world: "Civilized people of the world, come to our aid, not only with declarations but also with soldiers and arms! Don't forget that there is no other way to halt the wild onslaught of Bolshevism. If we perish, your turn will come . . . Save our souls!"

The United Nations met in emergency session in New York. It passed fourteen resolutions calling upon the Soviets to "desist from all attacks on Hungary." The Russian advance continued.

Janos Kadar, leader of the Hungarian Workers' Party since 1956 and presently Prime Minister of Hungary.

The insurgents' radio addressed the United Nations directly: "We beseech the world organization to dispatch prompt aid. We ask for parachute troops to be dropped in Hungary." In another plea: "Peoples of the world . . . listen to the cry of despair and give us your fraternal hand."

The fraternal hand was not extended. Soviet armor broke through the improvised defenses, gained control of the Danube bridges, the telephone exchanges, other vital public services. The Hungarian resistance began to fade away. The Nagy government was forced to abandon its post, finding temporary sanctuary in the Yugoslav Embassy of Budapest.

Four members of the government had left Nagy and turned up behind the Russian forces, forming a new "Hungarian Revolutionary Worker-Peasant Government." The leading personality in that cabinet was Janos Kadar, who had been a "Titoist" prisoner of the Rakosi regime. Kadar took over the government on November 4.

The insurgents' radio called: "Can the world let a small country lose its freedom?" On November 6, the government radio reported that "Fascist bandits" were still in combat, wrecking railway equipment. On November 7, a weak voice was heard from the insurgents: "Please forward our appeal to President Eisenhower . . . We are asking for immediate armed help."

Sporadic fighting flared up on the island of Csepel, at the Dunapentele heavy industrial centers; and guerrilla engagements continued in the Bakony hills and near the coal and uranium mines. While the armed resistance faded away, the workers' resistance continued, with many factory workers refusing to return to their plants. Production remained at a disastrously low level. The normal daily output of coal, one hundred and eighty thousand tons, fell to thirty-five hundred tons.

The uprising was over, however, and the casualties had to be counted. The government recorded twenty-seven hundred deaths; observers estimated the number at twenty-five thousand. Eyewitnesses reported trainloads of deported

Hungarians heading East. The U.N. special report on the insurrection noted: "No accurate figures exist about the number of deported Hungarians, but these certainly run into thousands."

While the fighting went on, some two hundred thousand Hungarians escaped to the West—about 2 per cent of the entire population.

In a sad epilogue, Imre Nagy emerged from the Yugoslav Embassy, believing that his safety had been guaranteed. It was not, and he was arrested and executed.

The peasants, although they undoubtedly sympathized with many of the aims of the insurgents, had played a limited part in the fighting. Villages and farms are widely scattered and hard to organize, and the uprising in any case lacked a central organization. Finally, while the peasants were unhappy with the Communist regime, they may have feared that its end would bring back the injustices of the prewar rule.

Few events of the decade aroused as much world attention as the Hungarian uprising of 1956. The Western press recorded it in amazing detail, in books as well as newspapers. The world became intimately acquainted with Hungary and the Hungarians, and learned to admire their gallantry.

The "gallant Hungarians" were now led by a government headed by Janos Kadar. Kadar was born in 1912 into a poor Hungarian family near the frontier of the country. He was too poor to have more than an elementary education. After leaving school, he worked as a locksmith, a streetcar conductor, a plumber, and an electrician. He fell under the influence of the Socialist young workers' movement, tending toward Communism, which was outlawed during the Horthy regime. Kadar was arrested and jailed for two and a half years. During World War II he joined the weak anti-German, anti-Horthy underground.

There were few native Hungarian Communists in those days; membership in the Party was looked on as a ladder to the gallows. When the Communists gained power after the war, these early "martyrs" had a tremendous advantage; if they were aggressive and bright, there were few positions they could not attain.

Kadar climbed very quickly. He became a member of the Political Bureau of the Party, then its deputy secretary general. But he fell under suspicion as a "nationalist" after Tito's heresy, and he was jailed and tortured. For three terrible years he was imprisoned.

With the post-Stalin "thaw," Kadar was released and readmitted to the party. He took a part in the revolt against Rakosi in 1956, but when Nagy moved to the revolutionary side he vanished from sight. Eventually he turned up in the van of the invading Russian forces, having formed a counter-government under Soviet protection.

Kadar's first task as head of the government was to put the country back on its feet. He could not count on the Western aid which had been available to Gomulka in Poland; he had to depend on the Soviets. It was in the Soviet interest to help Hungary, if only to prevent another explosion. The Russians provided the Kadar regime with a billion rubles worth of consumer goods, cancelled Hungary's long-term indebtedness, granted loans to the government, and shipped iron ore, coal, oil, and metals to Hungary.

Kadar changed the name of the Hungarian Communist Party to the "Hungarian Socialist Workers' Party." And where his predecessors had tried to make the Hungarians pro-Communist, Kadar simply asked that they not be anti-Communist.

Consumer goods were given high priority for the first time. Wages were increased, social services improved, vacation allowances liberalized. The political police were much less visible. The Hungarians, who love to grumble, were allowed a certain amount of verbal leeway as long as they did not question the basic policies of the regime. Some private enterprise was permitted, and the continuous propaganda was restrained.

In the early 1960's Kadar opened Hungary to foreign tourists, who could bring in the foreign currencies he badly needed. He also opened the frontiers to "reliable" Hungarians who wanted to travel, lightening the stifling atmosphere of a closed country.

Kadar's policies were not always in perfect accord with those of the Kremlin. The Russians were anxious to set up a Communist Economic Mutual Assistance and Cooperation Organization, known as Comecon. However, the satellite countries failed to heed the Kremlin's order to toe the economic line. They pursued their own policies with scant regard to the Comecon, which continues to exist though its effectiveness is limited. Kadar liked some features of Comecon, disliked others, and disclosed his views to the Kremlin. He did not want Hungary's development retarded by too-close association with the more advanced industrial countries. But he wanted Hungary industrialized as far as possible in order to gain higher living standards.

When the Kremlin deposed Nikita Khrushchev, Kadar wanted to be given some explanation. He did not eulogize the new Kremlin team. Also, he has taken steps to improve Hungary's relations with the West, particularly with the United States. He declared an amnesty for political prisoners and tried to encourage the 1956 emigrés to return.

The liberal policies of Kadar are closely related to the 1956 uprising. The Hungarian freedom fighters, though they were defeated by the Russians, won a measure of freedom for their country. Among the "Socialist Bloc" countries Hungary appears to be most relaxed. At the elections the monopoly of the "People's Patriotic Front" has been scrapped to give all qualified citizens the right to propose candidates for the local governing bodies and the national Parliament. Newspapers are again able to publish angry letters complaining about some of the government-run stores. People crack jokes at the expense of the government, as do entertainers on the stages of intimate theaters called "cabarets."

However, the Soviets kept the members of the "Socialist Bloc" under their thumbs. When Czechoslovakia attempted in 1968 to introduce its "New Model of Social Democracy," the Soviets feared the death-knell of their system in the area. Quickly, they organized an armed force, which Hungary and other Bloc countries were made to join, and invaded Czechoslovakia during the night of August 20. They crushed the Czechs' attempted democracy. Sadly, the Hungarians commented: "This shows again who is the cock in the eastern European barnyard." While the process of liberalization in their country continued, they knew how far they could go.

11

On the Farm and in the Village

HUNGARY has always been an agricultural country; nearly all of its land can be used for farming, and for centuries, Hungary has been the "breadbasket" of the Danube. Poets used to sing of her oceans of waving wheat, and an abundant rainfall in May was cause for national rejoicing. Farming is still important, but industry now shares its preeminence.

Hungary as an agricultural country has changed in several important respects during recent years. Along some rural sections of the Danube, the countryside seems almost lifeless. In the past, the peasants had hand tools which made them spend long hours in the fields. Now there are farm machines, requiring fewer hands and fewer hours.

Wheat was king in Hungary not long ago; today, a great

A typical village hamlet in the Lake Balaton region.

deal of land is devoted to corn and vegetables. Corn is raised to fatten the cattle; corn is eaten in the form of beef, with a high protein content and a higher price. Vegetables, too, bring a higher price than wheat. Rain in May is still important, but irrigation prevents the serious droughts which once brought famine.

The most obvious change in the Hungarian countryside is in the pattern of the farms. The checkerboard pattern of small farms surrounding huge estates has been replaced by large farming units which are owned and cultivated collectively. The Hungarians call such a farm *termelo szovetkezet*—producing cooperative society—and since that name is a tongue-twister even for Hungarians, they use an abbreviation: *Tsz*.

"Cooperative" gives an inaccurate impression; the farms are collectives like the Soviet *kolkhoz*. In a cooperative, the members retain rights to the ownership of the land they bring into it. They are there to "cooperate" with fellow-members in the performance of a common task, because they are thus able to operate more profitably. They can buy better machinery and get higher prices by eliminating the middle-man.

In a collective of the kolkhoz type, the farmer does not retain ownership to the land he brought with him; ownership rights are vested in the Tsz. The Hungarian peasant is supposed to receive a token payment for the land he owned, but the amount is small and is paid only for a couple of years.

Today, nearly all of the farm land of Hungary belongs to one of its thirty-five hundred Tsz. Occasional exceptions exist in the form of small pieces of land tucked away in inaccessible places, where private holdings could not be rounded out into large units.

However, tiny holdings are no longer profitable. The peasant could make a living on his small farm as long as farming was done by hand. He spent backbreaking hours with sickle, scythe, and hoe, but he loved his piece of land. Now machines have replaced hand tools, and new machines cannot be bought by small farmers, nor can they be used to advantage on tiny pieces of land.

The Tsz. can afford to buy expensive farm machinery far beyond the reach of the individual peasant. Large land holdings can benefit from irrigation and drainage; they can specialize in cattle breeding or truck farming or expensive and rare products. Under the new system, Hungarian farms have moved away from wheat to more profitable farm products. Employing scientific methods, they have specialized, introduced new products such as rice, and improved methods of cultivation.

The author recently visited a typical Hungarian collective near the town of Tura.

Tura, with a population of nine thousand, is situated on the banks of the Galga, a tributary of the Danube. The town is about thirty-five miles northeast of Budapest.

The collective has nearly five hundred and eighty members. Most of them live in town, which is only about a mile away from the farm. They commute on foot, on their bicycles, or on trucks. Many farmers, especially the young men, are being lured away to the big cities; 60 per cent of its members are women. The young men have gone to the capital to enjoy its bright lights, its theaters, its espresso shops, and its glamour.

The farms are short of hands, but so, too, are the industrial plants; Hungary has a laborer-shortage. The belief exists in America that workers in satellite countries are not allowed to leave their jobs. That is no longer the case. The regime cannot afford to restrain people from moving; unhappiness and dissatisfaction brings a decline in production. Farmers are free to move into the cities, and they do.

The Tsz. is run by "elected" officials, although the "election" seems empty to Americans. The official slate is presented to the members by the authorities, and it is voted in

After work at the tractor station of a collective farm.

by the community. Of course, the authorities try to offer an efficient and responsible slate; it is to their own advantage as well as that of the farmers. The technical manager on the sample farm near Tura is certainly a highly competent technician.

In every Communist country, production is carried out according to a plan which is worked out on the highest level of government. The farm is told the amount it is expected to produce, its "quotas" of corn, milk, vegetables, and to-bacco. The term "profile" is used for the principal products of specialization, and the plan for Tura has been given three profiles. Eventually it will specialize in one of the three, probably in cattle-breeding, which appears to be the most profitable for that particular soil, location, and complement of workers. One of its profiles is grain, the traditional wheat of Hungary and an ever-increasing acreage of corn to be used for fodder. Another profile is vegetables, to supply the inexhaustible appetite of nearby Budapest and other cities. Cattle breeding and dairying form the third, again made profitable by the proximity of Budapest.

Different regions have different profiles; in some areas, the soil fits the farms for the production of grapes. In Tokaj, for instance, the profile is wine, especially the dry *aszu,* wine of the first press. It is a highly respected profile, so much so that the vintner traditionally bows to the first barrel of the season.

On private farms the peasants raise their products, sell them, and live on the proceeds, plowing some of their earn-ings back into future production. On a collective farm, the members are paid according to a "work unit." A certain amount of work in a day is worth a certain amount of money; if a member performs more work, he gets more money. Work of a skilled variety is better paid than the simpler kind.

The operator of a harvesting machine gets payment for one "work unit" for his labors on, for instance, three acres. If he harvests six acres a day, instead of the standard three, he will be paid for two units. In certain professions, the worker is paid instead in accordance with the presumed importance of his task: a dentist is not paid for every tooth he pulls, nor a teacher for each student he teaches. These men are paid on the basis of an arbitrary number of work units per month.

The members of the Tsz. receive the usual social services as well as their pay: they have free medical care; they are looked after in ill health or old age.

Hungarians agree that the best feature of the system is the so-called "household allotment." Here the government has compromised with the peasant's desire to own his own land. Each of the members is allowed to have a small piece of land—usually an acre—on which he is king. This allotment may be next to his house or not, but wherever it is, it is productive. About 95 per cent of Hungary's egg production originates on these allotments, on which the farmer can raise his own poultry, a cow, and smaller animals.

The town of Tura is an overgrown village like thousands of other communities. These do not look alike, of course, but they all developed from the typical Hungarian village of the past, even of twenty-five years ago.

In those days, the rural areas were very backward. There were few paved roads. Consequently, the villagers were isolated during rainy weather, when the roads turned to bogs, and during the summer, when they choked up the traveler with dust. There was no electricity in the village, either. People went to bed early, and the village had a ghost-like look after dark.

Most of the houses were made of dried mud-bricks and thatched with straw. Many of the villages had no running water. A typical feature of the Hungarian countryside was the *gemes kut*—draw well—with an oaken bucket that could be lowered into the well by a system of poles and ropes.

The social life of the village centered upon the *csarda*, the tavern, filled with life and with the acrid smoke of cheap tobacco in old pipes. The owner dispensed the kind of wine Hungarians call *rabvallato*—"convict examiner," a means of torture to make the accused confess. It was a noisy place where everyone talked at once about farm problems and government. Sometimes a group of gypsy musicians came in, and then there was singing loud enough to raise the roof.

The Hungarian village looks very different today, since the autocratic regime has speeded up progress. The main street is paved; perhaps it is part of one of the national highways, traveled by the busses which crisscross the entire country. There are still unpaved side-streets, of course, muddy in rain and dusty in drought. Ducks and geese still waddle along beside them.

There are many new houses of cement and stone with roofs of red tile. The new roofs give shelter to storks and swallows, as did the old, but they may also hold the antenna of a newly-acquired television set. The village has electricity now, and running water. The bathroom, still a luxury, is no longer a miracle.

There is no typical Hungarian peasant architecture; the country has known too many invaders to feature only one style. The houses are usually low because height makes them hard to heat. Often their narrow side is turned to the street, with their wide front turned away from onlookers.

Hungarian countrymen love flowers and trees, and the village is scented by the sweet smell of the acacia tree. Flowers are on display around the houses, on the windowsills, and behind the fences—the most popular are geraniums, petunias, and mignonette.

Inside, the house is simple and functional, with space for knickknacks and works of art. Inevitably, there is a reproduction of a famous episode in the mid-nineteenth century war for independence: Kossuth on bended knee, praying for victory. There may also be a bust of *Kossuth apank*—our father Kossuth—the hero of his countrymen.

The house is full of religious and devotional objects, a crucifix in every room and at least one statue of the Virgin Mary, whom the Hungarians consider to be their patron saint. The authorities believe that religion is not popular in the satellite countries, but the farmers are still devoted to their church.

Often the bed in a peasant house is a family heirloom, made of heavy wood. The bedding is substantial, piled-up pillows and a warm eiderdown. Winter nights are cold, and a warm bed saves fuel. Outside the house is fixed a wooden bench on which the old people can sit and watch the sights of the village. Their serenity strengthens the visitor's im-

One of the new public libraries in Southern Hungary.

pression of tradition maintained in the fast-moving twentieth century.

The church occupies the center of town. It faces the main square, which is flanked by administration buildings and important shops. The square, which used to serve as a marketplace, is enlivened by religious processions on holidays and saints' days, despite the disapproval of the Communist party.

New in the villages are the Community Centers, which serve culture as well as propaganda. The Center is usually built around a large hall with a stage; attached is a public library. The hall is used for dances, political meetings, and hobby groups. It can become an auditorium for theater, movies, or lectures. The stage may be filled by a road company from Budapest, by Russian, European, or American films, or a lecturer interpreting the teachings of Karl Marx.

The public library is a real innovation. It serves propaganda, but it does much more. It is spacious, well arranged, well-lighted. The Communist classics are all there, but so are the classics of the rest of the world. Hungarian authors of an earlier day are cherished; so is Mark Twain, a great favorite whose books are available in Hungarian.

The csarda (tavern) is gone. It has been replaced by the pastry shop, which sells excellent sweets at moderate prices. The biggest business is ice cream, which seems to be the most popular dish in the village.

National dress is disappearing, sadly, although it reappears on festive occasions. Even the most backward Hungarian village responds to the dictates of Western fashion; the girls follow the fashions in dresses and hairstyles. Older women are generally dressed in black, and they always wear dark-colored kerchiefs on their heads. They still wear numbers of petticoats, especially to church.

In parts of the country where tradition is strong, national dress is still worn. In the West-Hungarian city of Sopron, women wear silk and velvet long skirts and aprons on festive occasions. The women of Kalocsa wear ribboned bonnets and tight bodices richly decorated with flowery designs. In Bodog, they wear embroidered white shifts and shoulder-covers. Towering, tiara-like bonnets decorated with pearls are flaunted in other rural areas. The many pet-

Festivals and holidays provide an occasion for dressing in the traditional costume of Hungary.

ticoats of Hungarian tradition scintillate in all the colors of the rainbow; the custom originated when rich fabric meant affluence. Women wore as many petticoats as they could, the better to "keep up with the Szabos."

In the old days, when peasants swung the scythe, they wore white linen leggings which left their legs unencumbered. Now there are no scythes, and no use for the leggings. Men now wear nondescript trousers and jackets of western style during the winter. In summer, they wear their trousers and an undershirt. A battered hat or Basque beret tops them off.

Another fast-disappearing feature of the Hungarian landscape is *cigany sor,* the Gypsy Row, as the government tries to resettle the gypsies among the rest of the population. The effort may not be successful, since the gypsies like their own ways and the rest of the people are prejudiced against them.

Hungary is right in the Gypsy Belt of Europe, which includes Rumania and other nearby countries. The gypsies can easily be distinguished from other Hungarians; they have swarthy skins, very dark eyes, and black hair. They speak Hungarian with a special intonation; many of them speak their own language. Scholars say that this language contains many words of Hindi, the national tongue of India. Some believe that India was the original gypsy home; others, that they arose in Egypt, and that "gypsy" is a twisted abbreviation of Egyptian.

Gypsies were among the distinguished company intended for extermination by the Nazis. Many of them were killed during the Second World War; but many others, aided by their nomadic tradition, successfully escaped capture.

Some of the best musicians in Hungary are gypsies. They seem to play naturally, without written music, with abandon and irresistible vivacity. The "name bands" of Hungary are often gypsy, and some of their band leaders are famous. The late Jancsi Rigo married a Belgian princess and became known throughout Europe.

Not all of the gypsies are musicians. They can be seen all over the Danubian area, peddling household utensils and repairing pots and pans for people who cannot afford to buy new ones. They make very little money, but they pay no rent; they live in their wagons, and keep moving.

Gypsy fortune-tellers, well known in the United States, are still seen in Hungary, but their occupation is not encouraged by the government. The authorities are trying to get young gypsies into school to learn a trade, but the success of the effort is uncertain.

The ancient traditions are still visible on the surface of rural life, but the transformation is basic. The old ways of life are gone except in relatively superficial aspects; the substance of life has undergone changes more profound than any Hungary has ever known.

In contemporary Hungary, American influence seems to be particularly strong. America's supermarkets are great hits in Hungary. Young Hungarians copy young Americans in many ways: in hair and dress styles, including the informal blue jeans; in dances and music. Almost anything from America is considered modern and therefore good. In many Hungarians' dreams there is an "American uncle," enormously rich—all Americans are supposed to be—leaving a vast estate to the kinsfolk in the "Old Country." Because there are so many uncles, cousins and other kinsfolk across the seas, to large numbers of Hungarians the United States is not only the strongest western nation, a superpower, but also an exported part of the homeland, and still more, a realized Utopia, far away yet tangibly near.

12

Folk Customs

ACCORDING TO an old proverb, the Hungarian is happiest when he is in tears. He wants music at weddings, at funerals, at religious and farm festivals, and much of his music is sad. Two great twentieth-century composers, Bela Bartok and Zoltan Kodaly, collected the songs of Hungary. Most of them are sorrowful, because the life of the poor man is sorrowful.

The outside world is more familiar with the gay songs of Hungary, or with the mournful songs brightened up by great composers. Everyone knows the ecstatic Hungarian rhapsodies of Franz Liszt and the dances set to music by Johannes Brahms. Hungarian tunes found their way into some of Beethoven's music and into the melodies of the King of

Girls in colorful dresses dancing the famous "bottle dance."

Operetta, Johann Strauss. The best-known composers of contemporary "Viennese" music, Franz Lehar and Imre Kalman, were both Hungarians.

Many of the folk customs of Hungarians are very old, so old that they originated when the people were pagans, nature-worshippers, before the coming of Christianity. These ancient customs are disappearing, but we can examine a few of them before they are gone.

Baptism is an important ceremony, and some of its attendant rites obviously pre-date the christening itself. The infant boy is supposed to become a good worker if an axe is left on his mother's bed during the ceremony; if the child is a girl, a spindle must be left on the bed to make her a good spinner. Dangers lurk in the dark, and a ribbon tied to the infant's ankles will keep away evil spirits. Nobody must admire the child's beauty for fear of arousing the envy of the evil ones.

On the day of the baptismal feast itself, presents are given to the child, and the feast itself is a picnic to which each guest makes a contribution. The godmother, whose responsibility is the greatest, comes to the feast weighted down with cakes and wine.

The baptism must be attended to without delay for an unchristened child may be exchanged for a devil's child before the ceremony. Such an infant is called a "changeling." An infant who dies before he is baptized is doomed to roam the earth, wailing miserably. He will appear in a bush or hedge every seven years; and when this occurs, a passerby must throw a white cloth on the image of the child. He then saves the child's soul by announcing: "I christen thee in the name of the Father, the Son, and the Holy Spirit. If thou art a boy thy name shall be Adam, and if thou art a girl thy name be Eve." The wandering soul then becomes an angel to whom the gates of heaven are opened.

Wedding customs are gay and exciting; most of them date back to the time when brides were bought or kidnapped. There were girl markets in remote parts of Hungary even early in this century, and there may be some still. In the old days, among the Ruthenians and Rumanians who lived in the mountains, the people lived in isolated families on small cleared patches of land; they did not see other families for months on end. They met only on market days when they displayed their goods for sale. They displayed their daughters at the same time.

Kidnapping customs survived for a long time after the last bride was kidnapped. All kinds of obstacles were placed in the way of the wedding procession, and the best man was called upon to perform difficult deeds and solve riddles.

"Wedding" is *lakodalom* in Hungarian, and the word also means "feast." The party lasts for days, sometimes for a week, and there is continual eating, singing, and dancing. All kinds of special dances, with special meanings, are performed by the guests and by the bride and groom. Jugglers perform their tricks, and a beautiful pageant may wind up the festivities.

Not only baptisms and weddings are gay; funerals are gay, too. Many of the peasants believed that life on earth is a sad and sorrowful business; that after death, the immortal soul of a man is transported to eternal bliss. The friends and relatives of the deceased mourn their own loss while they celebrate his happiness.

When a person dies, the window of his room is opened so that his soul may depart. The house is not cleaned nor kept warm while the body is there, because the soul should not be encouraged to return. A black flag flies in front of the house; candles burn in the windows. Neighbors arrive in groups; they praise the dead man's character, his courage,

A pilgrimage commemorating the centenary of the Proclamation of the Immaculate Conception.

and his kind heart. All night long, the relatives and friends keep a vigil.

Next morning, wailing for the dead begins. The melody of bereavement is ancient, and its words are traditional: "What were you to me? You were my everything, my life, my dearly beloved spouse. Off you went, leaving me all alone. Who is going to earn your poor orphans' daily bread, who is to provide them with clothes? Who is going to console your desperate widow? Who is going to tell me in the morning: 'Woman, do you hear the swineherd sounding his horn? The pigs are waiting at the gate. Drive out the sow.' Alas, alack, my poor dear husband, if I could only hear your stern words just once more, once again . . ." The female mourners, supported by professional "keeners," intone a rich collection of sad songs taken from hymns.

On the day of the funeral, mournful songs resound from early morning, when the procession begins. Neighbors walk in a long line, carrying the hoes with which they will shovel the earth onto the grave. The burial continues with much wailing and sobbing, but when the mourners return to the house of the deceased, the feast begins. There is a grand array of food and drink, and the guests begin to sing and dance as if they were at a wedding. They see it as a wedding, since their neighbor has become the bridegroom of Heaven.

Folk customs are intertwined with the farmer's year. In the old days, the fields of wheat were blessed so that "hail shall not destroy, the storm shall not ravage, and fire shall not consume the poor man's only hope." Each person returned from the field with an ear of wheat, to which, in some parts of the country, healing powers were attributed. The ceremony was held at the end of April, on the day of St. Mark.

The wheat harvest began on the day of St. Peter and St. Paul, at the end of June. On that day, the landowner was tied up with a rope of straw by the harvest girls, and he was released only for a ransom. There are no landowners now, and no ransom payment.

Secular harvest festivals occur all over the country. The

prettiest girl in the village is crowned Queen of Wheat, and she is sprinkled with water to insure a rich harvest. The reapers celebrate with colored gingerbread representing fine ladies, Turkish pashas, elegant hussars, and bouquets of flowers.

The vintage is a special time for Hungarians in the grape-producing regions; *"szuret,"* the vintage, also means "great" and "glorious." Long, dry summers ripen the grapes. Peasants visit the wine cellars which are built into the vineyard hills to sit around, look at the grapes, smoke their pipes, and drink a glass of "nectar." Suddenly, at harvest time, the vineyards hum with life. A gypsy band appears, and there is music and singing. Girls swarm around in their gay dresses. A procession of young horsemen gets under way, to swing through the town and end up at the village inn, where toasts are offered and everyone has a good time. This is the last farm festival of the year, followed by the quiet of the late autumn and the winter snow.

As young people move into the cities, peasant customs die out. In the cities, they forget their country songs and take up the latest fads in dance and music. In an era of global communication, the folkways of a particular region yield to the pressures of worldwide culture. The people's colorful traditions, in Hungary as nearly everywhere else in Europe, are yielding fast to the drabber but more practical ways of modern times.

13

Budapest—a Hungarian Rhapsody

WHAT MAKES Budapest so beautiful? The Danube, the graceful bridges, the mountains, the islands, the impressive buildings, boulevards, public parks? All of these, and more than these, because the city is wrapped in history.

The west bank of the Danube is hilly, and it is called Buda; the east bank, Pest, is on the plains. In Buda, one can imagine oneself in the midst of a mountain country; they seem to roll on to infinity. They stand guard over the Danube barely leaving a lane for the streetcar line. Gellert Mountain rises out of the river, its rocks supporting the old citadel from which one gets an incomparable view of the city, its bridges outlined at night by their shining rows of lights. Outlined, too, are the circular boulevards which go from the river back to the river again, and the enchanting islands of the Danube.

Romantic traces of history are everywhere. There is a monumental likeness of Bishop Gellert on the hill named for him, holding aloft a giant cross which can be seen from far away. The visitor is immediately reminded of the gruesome fate of this bishop, who was one of the missionaries brought in by St. Stephen to convert the Hungarians.

The divided city of Budapest, with Buda shown on the near side of the Danube.

Beyond a cleft in the range along the Danube is Castle Hill. The royal palace on the hill was shattered during the last war and is being replaced by an impressive cultural center. The side of the hill is adorned by the Coronation Church, in which Hungarian kings were crowned. In front of the church is a mounted statue of St. Stephen.

To the north of Castle Hill is a slender valley which serves a streetcar line, then another hill with the picturesque name of Rozsadomb, Hill of the Roses, its gentle slopes carrying pleasant country houses. Rozsadomb holds the tomb of a Turkish holy man, Gul Baba, and was a place of pilgrimage in the past.

Waves of mountains extend to the north and west, sheltering playgrounds and summer resorts and ski-trails. The tallest of them is called *Harmashatarhegy,* "three boundaries mountain," because it faces three counties.

The Danube at Budapest has just the right proportions, neither too wide nor too narrow, about five hundred feet in average width. If it were too wide it would dwarf the city; if it were too narrow, it would be crushed by its surroundings. Little steamers called "propellers" dart up and down the river.

The Danube bridges are its diadems; reconstructed since the war, no trouble or money has been spared to make them attractive, well-proportioned, and to make the new ones appropriate to the landscape. One of them, *Lanchid* or Chain Bridge, is well over a century old. Built by an Englishman, Adam Clark, it is the oldest suspension bridge in the world.

The most beautiful island of Budapest is Margaret's

The famous Chain Bridge connecting Buda and Pest.

Island; it has natural beauty, artificial beauty, history, and romance. The island is named for a daughter of King Bela IV, Princess Margaret, who in the thirteenth century became a nun in the convent on the island, her thoughts turned toward heaven by the horrors of the Tartar invasion. The ruins of the convent are still there, although they were ruined further during World War II.

In the middle of the island is a tremendous oak tree surrounded by a green meadow. In the shade of this oak, that most romantic of all Hungarian kings, Matthias Corvinus, took his afternoon rests after strenuous hunts. Not far from the tree is a rose garden which scents the island. Open air cafés, restaurants, a hotel, swimming pools, and a stadium have transformed it into a favorite summer excursion ground for the people of Budapest.

The eastern bank of the Danube holds a row of magnificent buildings. Parliament Building occupies the center of the Embankment, a vast Gothic structure with a huge cupola. At the approach to Chain Bridge is the Hungarian Academy of Sciences, a venerable structure. Before the Second World War, the famous *Korzo* was found on the Embankment. It was a promenade ground, flanked by hotels and cafés and brightened by the spirited tunes of the gypsy bands. The *Korzo* was demolished by war; its place has been taken by flower gardens, parks, and new buildings.

Most of the city lies behind the eastern embankment in Pest. It has become a large city, with a population of nearly two million, about one-fifth of the total population of Hungary. *Belvaros*—Interior Town—is old and dignified, with the best shops. Here and everywhere are scattered public parks, large and small, with flower beds and shady trees.

Beyond the old town is the core of Budapest, the residential and business centers. The devastation of war shows up here; the "skin" of the houses is peeling, and it would take tons of paint to restore the impression of youth. As darkness falls and the street lights are turned on, the blemishes on the houses disappear and the looks of the city improve.

War and revolution may follow one another, but city life goes on. Music is back, and so are the cafés. In Budapest, the cafés serve a variety of purposes. They are reading rooms for the large collections of newspapers, they are public salons where people meet to gossip and chat, listen to music, and watch their fellow-citizens. There was a time when cafés were used for the transaction of business, and they have been the workrooms of creative artists. Ferenc Molnar, the playwright, used his favorite Café New York as a writing room, observing his fellowman as he wrote about him.

Pest had a subway long before the city of New York had one; it was the first European capital to boast an underground railway. The subway remained stunted for many years, however, since surface transportation was adequate. The subsoil was found to be spotted with countless thermal wells, creating technical problems, and the cost of further work appeared to be prohibitive. But Budapest grew enormously, and the subway became a necessity. Its building was resumed, several miles added to the projected network, and work on its extension continues. Thus the earliest subway on the continent will not be one of the sketchiest.

Budapest grew faster than any other city in Europe, except Berlin. The Hungarians believed Chicago to be the fastest-growing city in the world, so they named a part of their own city "Chicago." The city was an exceptional theatrical center. At one time Hungarian playwrights provided plays for theaters of the world. In a single year in the mid-twenties, about a dozen Hungarian plays were performed on Broadway.

The prewar visitor to Budapest saw the cafés, the theaters, and the Korzo, but seldom realized that it contained one of the worst slums in Europe. The district

One of the many outdoor cafés in Budapest.

known as *Angyalfold*—Angels' Field—was filled with
tenement houses or "rent barracks." These miserable
houses had no running water, toilets shared by a dozen
flats, often one room inhabited by a couple of families. Many working people could not pay for a room, nor
could they pay for the use of a bed for the entire day. Instead they paid for its use during the part of the day in which
they were not at work; a day-worker used the bed at night,
a night-worker used it by day. If one of them fell ill, it was
just too bad.

Angyalfold is gone, and so are most of the other slums
in the capital. In the new housing projects are separate

baths for every flat; many of them have elevator service. Still there are slums, because people are moving into cities faster than housing can be built. At the present rate of urban growth it will be years before every person can have a room to himself.

Budapest is the largest industrial city of Hungary. The flour mills of the nineteenth century still flank the river; the city used to be second only to Minneapolis as a milling center. In the old days, boats from Russia and elsewhere deposited their cargo at the old grain wharves. Budapest is no longer exclusively a center for agricultural products; it is a center of industry as well.

Modern housing built to replace the old slums.

Iron works on the Danube.

The upper and lower reaches of the Danube at Budapest are flanked by factory chimneys. The factories turn out a large variety of consumer goods as well as capital goods—shoes, textiles, machines of all kinds, electrical appliances. Hungarian products have found markets all over the world, especially in the developing countries.

The largest industrial combine in Hungary is south of the capital on the island of Csepel. It has a working force of sixty thousand, its own railways and river craft, its own complicated industrial equipment. Industrial regions are cosmopolitan, and this one reminds the visitor of Pittsburgh rather than its own agricultural country.

According to the government, Budapest has too many industries now, and efforts are being made to establish new ones in hitherto-agricultural areas. The authorities hope to draw on the excess manpower of the countryside during winter, which is the slack season on the farms, instead of attracting more people to Budapest. This policy may be a wise one, but it will not be effective if the capital keeps on attracting farmers with its high wages, excitement, and entertainment.

The smoky chimneys of Csepel may not be as glamorous as the typical tourist's view of romantic Budapest, but they cannot be ignored. Sixty per cent of the national income of the country is provided by industry, and it is a twentieth-century truism that agricultural countries want and tend to become industrialized. Budapest, like other cities, is likely to become less glamorous and more businesslike as time goes on.

14

Urban Life

HUNGARIANS used to complain that "Asia begins at the outskirts of Budapest." This was never quite true, but certainly the village never reached a cultural level comparable to that of the capital. Hungarian cities, on the other hand, have an important place in European civilization.

Hungarian cities resemble Austrian ones; there is hardly any difference in the architecture. Urban civilization reached Hungary from the west, from Germany by way of Austria, with significant French influence. The cities are well provided with cultural institutions—with schools, museums, theaters, libraries, and concerts. There are public gardens and parks, swimming pools, and stadiums. There are open-air cafés, espresso shops, ice cream parlors.

By American standards, everything is on a small scale. Miskolc, for instance, is the second largest city in the country, yet it has only one hundred and seventy thousand inhabitants. It is considered a very large industrial center, yet all of its industries could be hidden in a tiny part of Pittsburgh. It has reached its relative importance through its location on the trunk line from Budapest to the Soviet Union. The city is situated in northeastern Hungary, not far from the Soviet border.

Miskolc has a little bit of everything, including history. In the Diosgyor suburb stand the remains of a castle known as the "Four Towers of the Queens," used by the wives of several Hungarian rulers. One of the houses in Miskolc is pointed out as the residence of Prince Rakoczi, the eighteenth century hero. In Hungary, places acquire fame if they were sites of a Kossuth speech or a Rakoczi headquarters.

Szeged lost its second place to Miskolc after the first world war, when its hinterland was assigned to Yugoslavia. The city lost its valuable raw materials and profitable markets, but it is still an important city with an impressive background. The house still stands where Kossuth delivered an historic oration on July 14, 1849. The Dome Square of Szeged is Hungary's most beautiful public square, presided over by the Votive Church erected in memory of the great flood of the Tisza river in 1879. The square, which accommodates five thousand spectators, serves as the auditorium of the Szeged Open Air Theater, the most famous in the country.

Hungary's third largest city is Debrecen, the "Calvinist Rome" in the heart of the Great Plains. The "Great

Church," dominates the center of the city. There Kossuth proclaimed the deposition of the Hapsburgs and the establishment of the Hungarian republic. The "Reformed College" of the city was the alma mater of some of Hungary's most important poets and statesmen.

Pecs, the "capital of Transdanubia," is in the southern part of the country and has a population of about one hundred and thirty thousand. The city is filled with reminders of Turkish times including three Muslim minarets, and it has a Christian catacomb which is reputed to date back to the earliest Christians. King Louis the Great founded its university about six hundred years ago; it is the fifth oldest school of higher learning in Europe.

The Calvinist Church in Debrecen, the "Calvinist Rome."

In Eger, too, there is plenty of history. In 1552, as we have seen, half of Hungary was under Turkish occupation. The Pasha of Buda, Ali, moved against the garrison at Eger with an armed force of some hundred and twenty thousand crack troops. The garrison-captain Stephen Dobo had only two thousand soldiers, but he was assisted by intrepid women who poured boiling pitch on to the heads of the Janissaries as they climbed the walls of the fortress. The siege lasted for thirty-eight days, and at the end, the Pasha had to retreat. Eger stayed out of Turkish hands for the next half-century.

Sopron, in western Hungary, goes back twenty-five hundred years. Under the name of Scarabantia, it was a Roman camp for four hundred years. Exposed as it is to western influences, Sopron adopted the most advanced European architecture, and even today it has many historic buildings, beautiful and valuable Renaissance, baroque and rococo edifices. The Storno House, today a museum, boasts that "King Matthias the Just slept here."

In any discussion of urban centers, our thoughts turn to industries and to education. Factories are the products of urban civilization. Schools are scattered, of course, throughout the country, but universities are found in the centers of population.

Factories employ more people than agriculture in Hungary today—1,800,000 as against 1,400,000. Considering the size of the country, Hungarian factories are large. They are owned by the nation and run by the government, for maximum efficiency. As a rule, large units are more profitable than small as cost declines with size.

A view of the ancient city of Sopron.

Hungary has had industries for a long time, but not of the kind or on the scale that she has them today. The flour mills on the Danube, the textile and sugar refining plants, employed the country's own natural resources. Hungarian technicians have long been excellent workers, and they have been turning out complicated machinery for a long time. Nowadays, business machines, electrical appliances, and metallurgical products are among the specialties, but the range of Hungarian products is very wide.

Like other Iron Curtain countries, Hungary had a planned economy. Preferences were established, quotas set, before the machines started. Planning brings advantages in efficiency and in reduced costs because competition, advertising, and salesmanship are eliminated. The planners never cease to remind the people that more is spent on distribution than on production in a capitalist society. Hungary moved closer to the capitalistic type of economy, however, by 1968. Until then prices of goods were fixed by government planners. Since then they have been set by supply and demand, in the usual Western way. Now the customer determines what should be produced. As a result, the Hungarians seem to live better. The Five-Year Plan, begun in 1970, is designed to increase consumer-oriented production on an even larger scale.

Looking ahead, the Hungarian government experts foresee a fourfold increase in the national income by 1980 (compared with 1960). During the same period, industrial output is expected to increase fivefold, while agricultural output will increase two and a half times. In the words of the planners in Budapest, "the consuming capacity of each individual in Hungary will be higher than in the fully developed capitalist countries."

The future sounds idyllic, but what about the present? How do the industrial workers fare today? In studying the answer to this question, one must not make the mistake of comparing Hungary with America. No country in the world has the living standards of the United States, and comparison is impossible and unrealistic. Besides, Hungary has always been a poor country with low average earnings.

A good salary for an average industrial worker in Hungary amounts to the equivalent of eighty dollars monthly, but it is almost impossible to make a meaningful comparison with an American pay-check. Not only does the *forint* vary in "official rate" and "free market rate"; it is difficult to determine just what the forint will buy. It buys next to nothing in luxuries, much more in necessities, and a lot in rent. The worker pays nothing for a wide range of social services provided by the state, although he must pay for them indirectly, of course.

Food is inexpensive in a restaurant and much cheaper in a factory canteen. City dwellers pay very little for rent; their landlord is the state rather than an individual. On the other hand, the purchase of a man's suit is quite an investment, and as a result, many Hungarians look shabby. Books are cheap, as are radios; a television set is expensive, and refrigerators are beyond the reach of the average family. An automobile is quite beyond the means of a Hungarian worker, but public transportation is cheap.

The average family of three spends 45 per cent of its income on food (including beverages and tobacco), more than a similar family in the United States. It spends nearly 7 per cent on rent, which is much lower than the American rate. Medical care and medicine cost nothing (directly), and the state pays vacation expenses for working people. Theater and opera tickets cost little for workers.

Most Hungarian factories are up-to-date, and an effort is made to make them attractive. There is a shortage of

Budapest. A "Közért" or self-service market.

An electroacoustical desk in a Budapest school helps children who are hard of hearing learn to speak correctly.

Science students at the Piarists Gymnasium of Budapest, a secondary school run by the Catholic Church which has been in existence since 1717.

laborers in Hungary, and there is competition among the employers (all representatives of the government) for the workers' time.

Laborers are issued working clothes by the plants; their shower rooms and restaurants are pleasant. The working day begins at seven or eight in the morning and lasts until four, and the workers are treated to tea or soda water on their "coffee breaks." Coffee is expensive in Hungary, but tea is imported from China and Indonesia at low prices. In mines and other "hardship" occupations, the working day is shorter.

An important grievance of the workers before 1956 was the amount of time spent on worker indoctrination. Nowadays, comparatively little time is spent on "brainwashing." The official newspaper is called the *Free People,* and the plant organizes "Free People Hours" for an hour every two weeks. Half of this time occurs during the regular work day, and the workers are paid for this portion of their time. At the meetings, an important editorial of the day is discussed; questions are permitted, and an attempt is made to answer them.

The factory management has extensive disciplinary powers. It can warn a man, demote him, or dismiss him. The worker may appeal against his management to a Committee of Arbitration on which management and employers are represented, and he may have recourse to the courts if he loses his first appeal. If he loses his case in the courts he will lose his job, but the shortage of laborers in Hungary makes this not a tragic event. As long as he is able and ready to work he will be employed, although perhaps at a lower wage and in a position of less prestige.

The cities are centers of higher education; the emphasis in Hungary is on natural sciences and technological skills. Foreign languages, particularly Russian and English or German, are considered very important. There is emphasis on the social sciences, which are taught in the Marxist-Leninist tradition.

The public school student must take mathematics every year. He takes six years of biology, five years of physics, and at least four years of chemistry. An attempt is made to introduce the student to technical skills by combining academic education with vocational training. Social sciences are taught very much like their counterparts in the natural sciences, despite the fact that in the western view, they are hypothetical while the natural sciences are concrete. In the Communist countries, educators maintain that there are constants in history like those in mathematics. If you know the basic factors of human institutions, you can regulate human behavior according to "laws" of social phenomenon.

The "general school" lasts for eight years and is compulsory for every child, entered at the age of six. The students attend for six days a week, six hours a day. Classes are held 213 days a year (180 in the United States). Homework is an important part of the curriculum and is expected to occupy most of the students' out-of-school time.

The child who does not go on to a secondary school must attend a part-time training school where he acquires a vocational skill. These schools are in session two days a week.

In Hungary, there are three main types of secondary schools, known as the gymnasium, technicum, and full-time vocational school. The gymnasium is an academic school, and its name is derived from a type of ancient Greek educational institution. Its emphasis is on liberal arts, to which are devoted five days a week. The sixth day is spent in the acquisition of technical skills; the combination is known as the 5 plus 1 program. The gymnasium is the most direct route to higher education.

The technicum is intended to train specialists in agriculture, industry, commerce, transportation, and public administration. Marxist-Leninist studies are built into the curriculum. Right now a "super-technicum" is in preparation, its students to be recruited from graduates of secondary schools.

Finally, the Hungarian system offers a full time vocational school. Two days a week are set aside to acquaint the student with the practical application of his studies; four days are devoted to the liberal arts.

Since 1956, when many young refugees came to America from Hungary, it has been possible to compare our educational system with the Hungarian on a basis of the results of both systems. American teachers have found the refugee children very well prepared indeed. The average Hungarian secondary school student had to absorb more mathematics than that required for admission to the Massachusetts Institute of Technology. In Hungary, as in Russia, in the words of Edouard Herriot, "Soviet rule bestowed on science all the authority of which it stripped religion."

Most of the schools of higher learning in Hungary are

called academies and institutes. A few of them, at Budapest,
Debrecen, Szeged, and Pecs, are called universities. There
are about fifty schools of higher learning, most of them
specializing in such subjects as medicine, dentistry, agriculture, horticulture, forestry, viniculture, natural sciences,
arts, and law. Polytechnic institutes prepare the students
for many branches of engineering; they have the largest
enrollment. Next come medical and pharmaceutical schools,
institutes of natural sciences, philosophy and, finally, juris-
prudence. It takes from four to six years to qualify as a
specialist in any of these fields—four years in agriculture,
five in engineering, and six years in medicine. Admission
to these schools is granted after obtaining a "maturity cer-
tificate" from a "secondary school," and, in numerous cases,
after passing an admissions test.

In the early years of the Communist regime only children
of the formerly "depressed" classes were admitted to higher
studies—children of peasants and factory workers. It was
these very people who played important parts in the 1956
uprising. Nowadays, students are admitted to the universities and institutes if they are sufficiently gifted, without
class discrimination.

The government provides scholarship grants to university students, the amounts dependent on their needs and
grades. The students are supposed to be allowed to devote
themselves to their studies without financial worries. Adults
who missed parts of their education in youth may resume
their education in factory schools or correspondence courses.

City life seems drab in comparison with the pre-war days,
partly because the people's clothes are drab, but it has its

compensations. Every Hungarian city has a playhouse for legitimate theater as well as movie theaters. Hungary has room for outings; it has the Danube and its tributaries for water sports, the mountains and hills, the parks, cafés and restaurants.

Hungarian boys cannot entertain their girls in the lavish style of young Americans. For an inexpensive good time, there is the Corso of every Hungarian city, which is thronged on weekends and holidays by hundreds of young people. At such times, the pastry shops and ice cream parlors do a booming business, and the tourist can see young Hungarians enjoying themselves in the manner of girls and boys all over the world. An increasing number of Hungarians spend their vacations abroad, especially in Italy, the "dreamland" of many people in the country. They are ardent mountain climbers in the Austrian, Bavarian and Swiss Alps. The traveling Hungarian from behind the Iron Curtain has become an everyday sight in other tourist centers of Europe, too.

The former Palace Hotel at Lillafured in the Bukk Mountains is now a labor union recreation home.

15

Epilogue

How ARE Hungarians faring today, not only as compared to their own past but as compared to other people's in the twentieth century? They talk fairly freely with visitors these days, and many of them grumble. However, Hungarians have always grumbled, and their complaints should not be taken at face value. A few of them are worse off than they were in the past; most of these are aristocrats or ex-members of the middle class, now vanished.

Most of the lower-class Hungarians could not be worse off than they were in the past and many of them admit that they are better off. The landless peasants and industrial workers used to earn starvation wages if any; they still earn very little, and their drab clothing reveals no prosperity.

154

But all of them can eat, all get free medical care, take vacations, and look forward to help from the state when they get old. Many of them have better housing than their parents. Too, their country's economy is being strengthened, and the time may come when the people's comfort will reflect higher living standards.

Hungarians are not members of a free democracy. Their representatives in parliament were handpicked by a clique. But then, the Hungarian has *never* been a member of a free democracy. If he was not ruled by alien masters, he was trodden under the heel of his own aristocracy, traditionally proud and inconsiderate, little concerned with the common people.

Janos Kadar, ruler of Hungary today, rose to his high position from the depths of Hungarian rural life. His behavior was reprehensible in 1956 but seems to have improved since, and under his administration the lot of the Hungarian common man has greatly improved. Most Hungarians feel that if their country has to be Communist, it could have a much worse leader than Kadar.

In foreign affairs, Hungary is too small a country to play an important role. Its fate will be decided by the Great Powers of today. It does not seem likely that the Soviet Union will let go of its satellites willingly as long as the cold war continues. The Russians have been twice threatened from the mid-Danube during this century, and after World War II they determined that this should not happen again.

However, Hungary and the other satellites are costly. Since 1956, Russia has had to invest millions of dollars in

Hungary alone, and she cannot be sure of Hungarian loyalty in any crisis. It would be very much in the interest of the Eastern European countries to see the cold war end and to see a readjustment in the European situation that would allow them to take their rightful place as independent nations once again.

In or out of the cold war, and whatever her circumstances, Hungary is not a country that will allow itself to be forgotten. With her intense love of liberty, her noble history, her rich land, and her brilliant, colorful people, she cannot be ignored in Eastern Europe or in the world.

For many centuries Hungary has been in Europe's storm center, and every inch of its soil has been watered with its patriots' blood. The "miracle" of Hungary is this: that a nation in an envied location and with no kin nearby has been able to hold onto its heritage for a thousand years. After so many sacrifices the Hungarians would like to enjoy their lives in peace. They know, of course, that this depends on the superpowers and not on themselves. Therefore, they watch the diplomatic scene intensely. They would like to see their country a flowering "bouquet" and not a mass of withered leaves.

INDEX

157